KENT·IN
OF·ART·&·DESIGN
LIBRARY

university college
for the creative arts
at canterbury, epsom, farnham
maidstone and rochester

Canterbury
New Dover Road
Canterbury
Kent
CT1 3AN

Tel: 01227 817314
Fax: 01227 817300
e-mail: librarycant@ucreative.ac.uk

The
Age of Louis XVI

The
Age of Louis XVI

Alvar Gonzalez Palacios

Paul Hamlyn

LONDON · NEW YORK · SYDNEY · TORONTO

Translated by M. H. L. Jones from the Italian original

Il Luigi XVI

© *1966 Fratelli Fabbri Editori, Milan*

This edition © 1969
The Hamlyn Publishing Group Limited
Hamlyn House,
The Centre, Feltham,
Middlesex

Text filmset in Great Britain by Yendall & Co. Ltd,
London

Printed in Italy by Fratelli Fabbri Editori,
Milan

For the history of art and manners the style which is usually called Louis XVI began some time before that sovereign came to the throne in 1774. Although Louis XV himself always preferred the style which today bears his name, Madame de Pompadour, his favourite, was not unaffected by the new trend in taste, of which there were already signs before she died in 1764. Her successor, Madame du Barry, was at once carried away by the new wave of enthusiasm for the Neo-classical, which she patronised and represented in her own home, the pavilion of Louveciennes, officially opened in 1771, which was entirely classical in style.

The events which led up to this new development may be traced, as with nearly all periods in European art, to Italy. There in 1738 the ruins of Herculaneum had been discovered, and in 1749 those of Pompeii, with the consequent well-known enthusiasm for archaeology. In 1750 the Marquis de Marigny, Madame de Pompadour's brother and the future Superintendent of Fine Arts, had left on a study tour of Italy, accompanied by three men who were already infected with the 'classical fever'; the engraver Cochin, the architect Soufflot and the critic Le Blanc. Marigny was not greatly impressed by the paintings at Herculaneum, finding them rather colourless, but he always had a great respect for the classical world and as a result was a good intermediary between Rococo and Neo-classicism. By that time the young Piranesi had already started his engravings of the magnificent ruins of Rome, and in 1769 he completed his *Diverse maniere di ornare i camini,* which greatly affected taste in decoration and certain furniture of the period and had remarkable affinities with the ideas of Robert Adam. The Comte de Caylus had published his *Recueil d'antiquités* as early as 1752, which later influenced many decorators and even inspired actors' costumes. Then in 1762 Mengs' reflections on ideal beauty appeared, followed two years later by Winckelmann's important writings. Both these men lived in Rome, where the French Academy had an establishment in the Corso where young French artists were sent. Thus Vien, David and many of those responsible for establishing the Neo-classical style spent their formative years in Rome, in close contact with the world of artists, critics and antiquarians, among whom were painters like Pompeo Batoni and Gavin Hamilton. Above all there was Antonio Canova, who was to become the greatest sculptor of his time, finishing in 1781 his first masterpiece, *Theseus and the Minotaur,* which was partly the result of his conversations with a pupil of the sculptor Coustou, one Quatremère de Quincy who became a very influential critic, especially after the Revolution.

The connection between this hive of cultural activity and the beginnings of a new fashion in interior decoration in France are easily understood, but difficult to pinpoint. The effect was soon seen in Paris. Lalive de Jully, for instance, a famous collector, furnished a *cabinet* in the 'Greek' style in 1758. The rather heavy Neo-classical pieces were designed by an architect, a pupil of Piranesi; a portrait painted for the collector by Greuze a year later, which is now in Washington, gives some idea of it. Not long afterwards a publicist called Eberts had the inspiration to invent a large perfume burner copied from a picture by Vien which he called *at hénienne* after the title of the painting. The Louis XVI style was born; from then on there were countless pyramids, columns, medallions, urns and sarcophagi; from hairstyles to furniture, soup tureens to the decoration of snuffboxes, everything was *à la grecque* or more generally *à l'antique*.

But there were other factors besides these to be taken into consideration. Anglomania, for example, introduced into French elegance a note of sobriety which although somewhat insipid, married exquisitely with the grandiloquence of the high fashion. The atmosphere had changed, and was changing all the time. Where previously there had been a reverence for the pastoral—the flocks, streams and rustic life of Boucher's pretty affectations—now a new realism emerged inspired by avid reading of Rousseau, while attitudes of severe stoicism conditioned philosophical thinking to the passing of things human. Gradually Madame de Pompadour's cultural pastimes gave way to the academic preoccupations of Madame de Staël, the gallant smile of Jean

1. Elisabeth Vigée-Lebrun (1755-1842). *Marie Antoinette and her Children*. Versailles.

1.   Elisabeth Vigée-Lebrun (1755-1842). *Marie Antoinette and her Children.* Versailles. The artist was one of the most famous portrait painters of the period. For this picture her colleague David advised her to take inspiration from a Madonna by Raphael, and the pyramidal composition is reminiscent of of the great Italian's work. In the background on the right is the famous jewel cabinet by Bélanger, which no longer exists.

2.   Marie Antoinette's cabinet doré at Versailles. Although the room was built under Louis XIV this typically Louis XVI decoration was finished in 1783 by the Rousseau brothers. Most of the furniture is now dispersed but the room has been refurnished with pieces of the period. The fireplace and chandelier are the originals; in the former the caryatids in classical style are especially interesting. The chased gilt bronze chandelier has been attributed to Gouthière.

3.   Mantlepiece in Marie Antoinette's boudoir at Fontainebleau. The mantle is decorated with bronzes representing a bow threaded with garlands of flowers. The two side pieces are in the shape of quivers. The elegantly chased andirons are decorated with little classical urns. Above is a mantle clock on little columns and two candelabra in the style of Clodion.

2.   Marie Antoinette's cabinet doré at Versailles.

3. Mantlepiece in Marie Antoinette's boudoir at Fontainebleau.

Honoré Fragonard to the impassivity of David.

It is curious that this seriousness was not found at all in the distinguished circles of the court. Louis XV's last years were disastrous, and Madame du Barry certainly did not compare well with her forerunner in the King's favour. As for Marie Antoinette, she had neither the intelligence of Madame de Pompadour, nor the casual flair of Madame du Barry, and her taste was far from dependable. She was easily dazzled by anything new and rarely showed that she was capable of distinguishing what was worthy of encouragement. She never lost a certain Germanic stolidness, and appeared to have neither discernment nor any real interests except for a love of flowers, absurd exaggerated headdresses by Leonard, extravagantly luxurious clothes by Rose Bertin, bright, cheerful fabrics and a passion for her innumerable beribboned cows which she foolishly amused herself by milking in her various dairies. Her epitaph is famous: 'Why don't they eat cake?'. If that is not proof enough, her mother wrote to her in this vein when her intelligence—or lack of it—was still not fully apparent: 'You have quickly gained the affection and devotion of everyone. Do not discount the reason for it—not your beauty, which is nothing out of the ordinary—nor your talent or your knowledge, you well know how little you have of either, but the goodness of your heart. . . It is said that you forget to treat the nobles of the country with the respect due to them and that you do not talk to them, but chatter with the youngest ladies in your retinue and play all sorts of silly games.' Her brother

Joseph II had much the same sort of thing to say.

Louis XVI himself, the 'bonhomme' (fellow) as his royal consort used to call him with unjustifiable contempt, was passionately fond of hunting and clockmaking and full of good intentions—a trait somewhat balanced by more than a fair share of weakness. The only member of the royal family to show more than a casual interest in Neo-classical art was perhaps the Comte d'Artois (who many years later as Charles X was one of the most stupid sovereigns in the history of France). In fact his little château at Bagatelle was one of the most representative ensembles of the age.

Fortunately the Marquis de Marigny was succeeded by an equally sensible man, the Comte d'Angiviller, who secured some very beautiful objects for the various royal residences, which nevertheless did not have any definite style during this period as they had had during the reign of Louis XV. This was not for lack of enormous sums of money being spent to equip the palaces; on the contrary, at least until 1785, when the financial deficit assumed alarming proportions, the Crown continued to squander, as never before, entire fortunes on acquisitions of every kind. Despite the fact that Necker with unparalleled optimism had thought he could conceal the imminent bankruptcy, no one believed his famous *Compte rendu au Roi,* to the extent that it was nicknamed the *conte bleu*—a sailor's yarn. . .

But time never stands still: there is a continual state of flux and innovation, and everything political and artistic is subject to change. That particular period defies any precise definition. If on the one hand the Encyclopedists and philosophers responsible for the Revolution to come were basically conservatives, as many historians have thought, on the other hand men as diametrically opposed as Fragonard and David were contemporaries. This dynamic spiritual diversity, this *Weltanschauung,* in many ways so close to that of the 20th century, logically enough affected all areas of knowledge and fashion even in the most humble ways, like the coffee cup painted one day with the symbols of monarchy and the next with the tricolour and the *bonnet rouge* of the Republic.

Another important factor was the cultural supremacy of the French throughout Europe. In every field of art and knowledge France enjoyed the highest prestige, even for the language, 'which', wrote the King of Poland, Stanislas II Poniatowski, 'every young man in Europe learns as a sign of his education'. The only country which offered any competition was Italy, and then only in the artistic field. Thus it was that at the Polish court Poniatowski only wanted French or Italian artists like the architect Victor Louis or the landscape artist Bernardo Bellotto. There was constant competition among the northern sovereigns to secure the best pieces when a Parisian collection came up for sale. Catherine the Great of Russia, thanks to the advice of Diderot and Grimm, nearly always had the prize pieces. Her correspondence constantly refers to possible acquisitions favoured by the death or bankruptcy of some connoisseur, or to works commissioned from the factories of Sèvres and Gobelins, or from the most famous artists. Often these Parisians of the north showed more discernment than the nobles of the court in Paris. Madame du Barry for some unknown reason never wanted Fragonard's 'Grasse' panels, but Poniatowski did not hesitate to secure for himself one of the best paintings of the artist's later years *Le Baiser à la Dérobée*. The King's favourite spent more than £430 for Gouthière bronzes, while Catherine the Great for only £265 purchased the whole Crozat collection, one of the most important of the whole century, which formed the basis of the Hermitage collection. From it du Barry had foolishly only chosen one painting, the portrait of Charles I of England by van Dyck, now in the Louvre, and even then she had not selected it for any artistic reason, but because she wished to flaunt her alleged descent from the Stuarts. However, she did at least buy a few important paintings and patronise artists of some merit, which is more than can be said of Marie Antoinette. Her collections consisted of Japanese lacquers, petrified woods, mounted cameos, a few pieces of good furniture, and the most un-interesting portraits by Drouais or Madame Vigée-Lebrun, all of which were no doubt delightful, but there was hardly a single outstanding work among them. Even these collections of precious oddments show her lack of originality; the Duc d'Aumont before her had collected lacquers and semi-precious stones, the Prince de Condé had had picturesque gardens, and the English had installed hygienic

4. Detail of the *boiserie* of Marie Antoinette's cabinet doré at Versailles, 1783.

5. Pierre Gouthière (1732-1813/14). Perfume burner.
Wallace Collection, London.

4. Detail of the *boiserie* of Marie Antoinette's cabinet doré at Versailles. 1783. The *boiseries* of this room were designed by the architect Mique, carved by the Rousseau brothers and gilded by Dutemps. The recurring motif consists of a smoking perfume burner flanked by two sphinxes back to back, which is often found in Neo-classical art. Their tails curl round the tripod, and on their heads rest delicate flowering shoots.

5. Pierre Gouthière (1732-1813/4). Perfume burner. Wallace Collection, London. The red jasper vase which forms the basis of this object has provided a marvellous foil for the artist's creation of an exquisite tripod in gilt bronze, worked like a jewel. Each leg is finished with a satyr's mask at the top and rests on a small jasper base. In the centre a serpent coils from top to bottom.

6. Louis XVI clock. Private collection, Milan. This is a good example of a clock in French Neo-classical style: the curving base rests on typical top-shaped feet. From this rises the straight central part, with two upturned brackets on either side. The top is decorated with a miniature perfume burner decorated with ram's heads. The gilt bronze decorations represent ribbons, bows and laurel leaves.

7. Louis XVI ornamental statuette. Private collection, Paris. This finely finished gilt bronze statuette is one of a pair; they were usually placed either side of a mantlepiece or on a console table. This one probably represents one of the muses, and is an example of the fashion for mythology of the period with its didactic symbolism. The costume, as always, is taken directly from classical art.

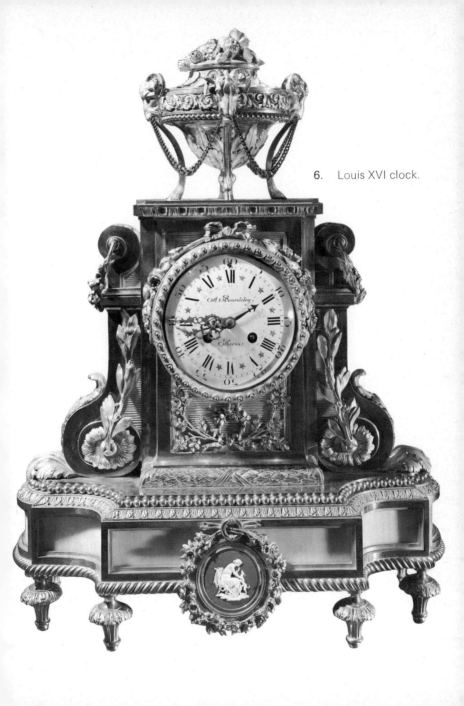

6. Louis XVI clock.

7.   Louis XVI ornamental statuette. Private collection, Paris.

lavatories before she did at Versailles (where they were in fact called *à l'anglaise*). She never wanted to own a Fragonard or a Houdon, nor was she to be painted by David, except on the executioner's cart; but she was involved in a serious scandal because of a necklace. Her taste was really, as Verlet leniently declared, '*le goût tapissier*'.

Exoticism was still fashionable. As soon as a Turkish deputation arrived Vigée-Lebrun rushed to have a look, so that she could paint her mother dressed as a sultana; and when the Indian envoys of Tippoo Sahib came to Paris in 1788 she was determined they should pose for her. What is more, all society went mad about them: the Duchesse de Chartres received them at the Palais Royal and their likenesses in coloured wax were exhibited to the public in the Cabinet de Curtius. The Queen had a 'Turkish' room made for her, from which comes a curious divan now in the Musée des Arts Décoratifs, and the Duc de Chartres put up a minaret in the gardens at Monceau. Even the fashion for *chinoiserie* did not seem to be on the wane: the Chinese baths were much frequented in Paris, even by those most in the public eye, and there was a shadow theatre in the *Redoute chinoise,* a café renowned throughout Europe. Even the gardens were transformed into miniature oriental forests, scattered with pagodas and little temples, especially after the book on the subject by the English architect William Chambers had been translated into French. There was an oriental footbridge in the garden of the Princess of Monaco at Betz which was guarded by winged dragons with three heads, whose fearful bell-teeth rang in the wind.

These were the things that France borrowed, but she gave generously in return, filling the luggage of every visitor with the countless new trinkets that fashion dictated every season, like the all-white toilet sets which were the rage in 1782, perhaps because of the influence of the Creoles, or the complicated hairstyles designed to celebrate a victorious ship. Those who were unable to go to Paris in person had dolls sent to them, dressed down to the last detail, so that even from a distance they might choose the latest and most enchanting clothes and accessories.

The wind of change blew through theatrical circles too. Mademoiselle Clairon had complained even at the height of the Rococo period of having to play Electra in a pink dress with black jet trimmings, but it was not until the actor Lekain decided to don a toga that things began to change. Even he could not relinquish the plumes on his headdress or remove his silk stockings. It was the singer Madame de Saint-Huberty who finally made a clean break and appeared in entirely 'Grecian' dress in Spontini's *Dido* in 1783, wearing a peplos, and in the following year in Gluck's *Iphigenia*. Hellas triumphed, bringing with it the cleanness and healthiness which the art of the time seems to have, and which is the subject of the 'Ode to the salubriousness of the air' by the Italian Giuseppe Parini. It is surprising that art and poetry were not inhibited by these academic exercises.

Before concluding this short introduction it is worth remembering that at least at Versailles the Revolution had more respect for the flourishing art of Bourbon France than is usually believed. The statues of the 'despots' were destroyed, some châteaux were burnt and many of the things which had filled the royal palaces were disposed of indiscriminately. But the barbaric excesses of many of the 19th-century financial companies were yet to come. Even now, and not only in France, there is a risk that far more is being destroyed. Often the revolutionaries were content to strike out the symbols of monarchy, or to remove the head of Louis XVI from a statue and transform it into a goddess of charity, as happened in the bas-relief at the School of Medicine, or to give a Virgin a *bonnet rouge*.

When on 21st January 1793 the severed head of the *citoyen* Capet rolled to the ground, at least everything, or nearly everything, had already been stated as far as art was concerned. The Consulate and the Empire in the beginning only reworked that inheritance; Houdon, David and Jacob had said what they wanted to say, and a new generation was needed before any profound changes could be seen. Not that one should reject the famous saying of Goethe who saw in the battle of Valmy the end of the *ancien régime* : 'In this place and on this day starts a new era in the history of the world.' It was just that for the history of art that day fell some years later.

PAINTING

Boucher's porcelain-tinted paintings have a grace which is peculiarly French. His exquisite taste might be that of a master of haute couture, his wit is deliciously Parisian, but if one imagines the effect these works had on Fragonard, a man from the Midi, with his riotous imagination and his unbridled natural strength, then one can begin to have an idea of the importance of the art of Fragonard for 18th-century Europe.

L'aimable Frago, as he liked to be called, was born at Grasse, in Provence, and although his family soon moved to Paris, the southern breezes were to call him for many years to come. He had the same apprenticeship as many French painters of the time: he was a pupil of Chardin first, then of Boucher and of van Loo, and in 1755 he was already at the French Academy in Rome where he stayed until 1761. While there he enjoyed among other things the friendship of the Abbé de St Non. His years in Italy definitely left their mark on him, unlike many other artists, Greuze for instance, who despite long stays in Rome understood very little, not of what they saw, but of the essence of the Italian spirit. Strangely enough the painters who seemed to capture his imagination most were the Genoese. He must have seen and liked the brilliant creations of Gregorio de Ferrari, whose lively colour schemes and sense of 'grand décor' were well suited to his own uninhibited enthusiasm. Natoire, at that time director of the Academy, made him copy paintings by Pietro da Cortona, but when he was on his own, both during this first visit and during his second Italian stay, he lingered profitably in front of Luca Giordano's frescoes and Solimena's rich black and brown shadows.

Fragonard used to spend whole days at the Villa d'Este at Tivoli, and his drawings describe his romantic walks through the damp shady gardens, beneath the soft pinnacles of cypress trees, past limpid waterfalls spilling from the mouths of stone lions into ancient porphyry basins. These moods of enchantment can only be understood by those who love Italy but were not born Italian. There is a happiness in the red chalk drawings, so full of elegance and movement, which is the expression of his ardent heart, and a happiness in the leaves drawn so finely with the fleshy tip of his finger that they might have been done with a butterfly wing. In Paris his youthful, sensuous ardour was appreciated more by the connoisseurs than by the court. Unfortunately he only met Madame de Pompadour just before her death, and although Madame du Barry, her successor in the King's favour, did acquire some of his paintings for the Pavilion of Louveciennes she rejected the panels dedicated to the *Progress of Love* which are the most exquisite and enchanting works that Fragonard ever painted. The artist rolled them up and for many years kept them in his studio, until the Revolution was well under way, when he decided to hang them, together with other extraordinary creations, in the drawingroom of one of his cousins in Grasse. It was only at the end of the 19th century that they were removed from there to be given a permanent home in America.

Two memorable pictures of slightly later date are the *Fête de St Cloud,* painted for the Duc de Penthièvre, now the property of the Banque de France, and the *Fête à Rambouillet,* owned by the Gulbenkian

27

Foundation, where the vegetation spills out like a firework or a solid shower of golden rays. A golden ship gay with ribbons and streamers rides through a foam of enchanted waves, a stream falls in clear sparkling sprays into the valley, and above the curtains of greenery at the top stands a solitary tree, gnarled and leafless, as though struck by love's lightning. But Fragonard also painted the joys of motherhood. He was the poet of young lovers who write their sweetheart's name on a tree trunk.

It does not matter that his fantasies should sometimes be called obscene. 'His decency lies in the delicacy of his colours,' the Goncourt brothers aptly commented. No highly moral-minded person could understand better than Fragonard the cunning innocence of children. He managed to blend emotion and amusement unusually successfully in his little groups of governesses with their tiny golden-haired, half-naked pupils, who learnt to read from slates larger than themselves, or who played at teaching their little dogs (*Education is All*). The art of Fragonard might be described as popular, and may have been influenced in the beginning by Chardin; but the latter's feeling of pious impassiveness has been abandoned, and a taste for the picturesque and for genre scenes prevails. It corresponds in painting to the custom of the time for the *fantaisies campagnardes,* which took place, for example, in Marie Antoinette's hamlet.

So far Fragonard still seems to fall within the classification of Rococo or, to use a convenient label, the Louis XV style, despite the fact that his activity falls chronologically into the early Neo-classical

8. Louis Léopold Boilly (1761-1845). *The Gohin Family*.
1787. Musée des Arts Décoratifs, Paris.

9. Hubert Robert (1733-1808). *Imaginary View of the Port of Ripetta, Rome.* 1766. Ecole des Beaux Arts, Paris.

10. Jean Baptiste Greuze (1725-1805). Sketch for *The Village Betrothal.* Petit Palais, Paris.

8.   Louis Léopold Boilly (1761-1845). *The Gohin Family.*
1787. Musée des Arts Décoratifs, Paris. This is one of the most
successful pictures by this delightful genre painter, whose
canvases reveal much about the society of the period. The
clothes are already in the more modest taste of the late 18th
century, and the furnishings comfortably simple. Particularly
interesting is the roll top desk at which the portly father
of the family is sitting, wearing a wig which was by that time
out of fashion.

9.   Hubert Robert (1733-1808). *Imaginary View of the
Port of Ripetta, Rome.* 1766. Ecole des Beaux Arts, Paris.
The artist has excelled in this imaginary view where fantasy
is based on reality, imagining the Pantheon near the Tiber.
The canvas is filled with a suggestively lyrical rosy light. The
figure half way up the steps is similar to Piranesi's work.

10.   Jean Baptiste Greuze (1725-1805). Sketch for *The
Village Betrothal.* Petit Palais, Paris. Greuze's art, which
played a more important part than is usually admitted in
setting the Neo-classical trend, seems to stem from a rather
conventional hypocritical piety. The actual quality of his
painting, his strict compositions and his narrative genius
should be accorded the merit they deserve.

11.   Jacques Louis David (1748-1825). *Paris and Helen.*
1788. Louvre, Paris. This is one of David's works which was
most in tune with the elegant, lifeless and decorative taste of
Neo-classical France. Contrary to the *Oath of the Horatii,*
which is the result of his attempts to achieve a controlled
vigorous style, this is perhaps the most brilliant example of
the so-called *genre agréable* intended to show a more gentle,
pleasing side of classicism.

11. Jacques Louis David (1748-1825). *Paris and Helen.*

period. However from 1780, as though he realised that the temperature had fallen, he tried desperately to modify his bizarre exuberance to suit the dignified calm and reserve of the day, and he did so extremely gracefully. Critics have often commented on the decadence of these last works, but paintings like the *Sacrifice of the Rose,* or the *Fountain of Love* cannot be called second rate. On the contrary Fragonard seems to have melted the ice of Neo-classicism with a note of romantic grace, and the quality of the painting itself is still beautiful. If it no longer has the creamy porosity which Renoir tried to imitate a century later, it has acquired a silky sheen which in its own way is equally enchanting. This applies to the little compositions on which he collaborated with his sister-in-law, Marguerite Gérard, and to the little masterpiece *Le Baiser à la Dérobée* (Hermitage, Leningrad), the prototype of all the Boilly paintings and a perfect example of the taste and civilisation of an epoch.

A Grandfather Reading the Bible to his Family, The Mother, The Paralytic Tended by his Children, The Good King, The Grandmother, The Father's Curse, The Nurse's Return—one only has to look at the titles of some of Greuze's paintings, aptly chosen by him, to understand the intentions of this sentimental and rather equivocal moralist, who had an unprecedented success in his own day, comparable only to Boucher's. Countless critics, starting with the Goncourts, have drawn attention to the moral purpose and rather conventional insincerity of Greuze's paintings, with their sickly triteness, the constant desire to teach a lesson, and to demonstrate the beauty of work, poverty and humility. But he could not help adding a certain *chic* to his poverty: a virtuous soul raising her eyes to heaven reveals at the same time her rosy bosom, despite the transparent veil which conveniently covers her. Not only have his labourers never worked in their lives, but they would not know how. His interiors are the interiors of the *opéra comique*, his urchins are Boucher's cupids without wings and rose garlands—in fact often his paintings are very reminiscent of *tableaux vivants*. It is also true that to publicise his painting *The Widow and the Parish Priest* Greuze wrote long letters to priests, or as he called them the 'protectors of religion and morals'. But if for a moment one can discount this unattractive element, his pictures appear in a new light. Greuze was after all a true son of his time. His work was the natural consequence of the aesthetic ideas of Diderot, for example, and a living illustration of the humanitarian propaganda of the philosophers, although the artist probably never understood it very well, nor even believed in it. Bearing this in mind one is immediately struck by his intelligent compositions, based on models by 17th-century masters like Le Nain and, in one painting at least, by Caravaggio. *The Broken Mirror,* now in the Wallace Collection, London, is like the Doria *Mary Magdalene* treated on a bourgeois level. The actual quality of his painting is equally impressive, for although he never attained the heights of Watteau or Fragonard, as his incredible vanity had led him to hope, his work nevertheless has unusual dignity. As a draughtsman on the other hand, he had moments of real inspiration and could convey genuine emotion, as in the very beautiful *Head of a Young Man* in the Hermitage, which Delacroix would have appreciated for its latent Romanticism. His studies of children need no justification. Even the Goncourts, who certainly cannot be said to have had much time for Greuze, were of the opinion that 'the charm of Greuze, his vocation, his originality and his strength are only really apparent in his studies of children. These alone compensate for all the weakness, poverty and insincerity of his glossy larger canvases.'

Hubert Robert spent eleven years in Italy, where he used to sketch the ruins, drink in the pink and gold sunsets of the Pincio, study the elegant spreading trees of the Roman campagna, and meditate in those places which had been dear to Claude. Robert's works were much admired by his contemporaries and are equally successful today, for they are neither rhetorical nor excessively sentimental—his approach to nature is sympathetic and his passion for ancient ruins is half way between the tourist's and the pilgrim's. The spontaneity and freshness of his style have a delicacy and decorative appeal which never seems repetitive or commonplace. He was doubtless able, while in Rome, to study Piranesi who at that time was involved in glorifying the magnificence and grandeur of Rome in his dramatically forceful etchings, where the ink looks as though it has been split haphazardly over the pages, creating breathtaking effects of light and shade. Piranesi's work verges on the tragic in its majestic feeling for time and space and in the shadowy consistency of the figures, like corpses or ghosts unearthed from some colossal buried world.

12. Jacques Louis David (1748-1825). *A Man with the Plague*. 1780. Ecole des Beaux Arts, Paris.

13. Jean Honoré Fragonard (1732-1806). *The Shady Walk.*
Petit Palais, Paris.

14. Jean Honoré Fragonard (1732-1806). *Madame Bergeret de Norinval.* Musée Cognacq-Jay, Paris.

12.   Jacques Louis David (1748-1825). *A Man with the Plague*. 1780. Ecole des Beaux Arts, Paris. This drawing is a study for one of the artist's early paintings, the *St Roch* at Marseille, painted in Rome in 1780 when he was studying Valentin and Caravaggio.

13.   Jean Honoré Fragonard (1732-1806). *The Shady Walk*. Petit Palais, Paris. The drawing here becomes a statement of a perfect poetic image. Few were able to capture so exquisitely the shimmering light and moist shadows of the paths, and the luxuriant foliage of the trees.

14.   Jean Honoré Fragonard (1732-1806). *Madame Bergeret de Norinval*. Musée Cognacq-Jay, Paris. The gracefulness of this painting, with an underlying tension, brings Fragonard even nearer to the rather delicate sensibility of pre-Revolutionary France.

15.   Jean Honoré Fragonard (1732-1806). *The Bathers*. Louvre, Paris. This painting shows the Rococo side of the artist, when he not only lets himself be carried away by his sensually joyous imagination but almost seems to paint with succulent brush strokes. The influence of Boucher and, above all, of Rubens is particularly evident in the paintings of this phase.

16.   Jean Honoré Fragonard (1732-1806). *The Washerwomen*. Musée de Picardie, Amiens. This is Fragonard at his most Italian. The marble statue seems almost transparent in its rough outline; nearby the lion spills a stream of water, and the women seem to speak in undertones in order not to wake their masters.

15. Jean Honoré Fragonard (1732-1806). *The Bathers.*

16. Jean Honoré Fragonard (1732-1806). *The Washerwomen*. Musée de Picardie, Amiens.

The limpid elegant canvases of Hubert Robert, on the other hand, are graceful and serene, radiant with soft pink and yellow light. He must have seen some of Pannini's views, which are very French in style, because he had the same habit of grouping different monuments together in a more or less arbitrary way, creating new squares and corners which have their own bizarre and fantastic reality. His love of ruins carried him to other extremes, such as visualising existing buildings like the Louvre in ruins; in fact this *ruinisme* was one of the most common aspects of the late 18th-century return to antiquity. Next to Hubert Robert comes Joseph Vernet of whom Diderot has left a vivid account in his *Salon* of 1767, where he describes Vernet's landscapes as though he were referring to real places, thus emphasising their 'reality'. But Vernet's landscapes, and especially his seascapes, were not so realistic and are more fascinating for their enchanting and picturesque decorative sense which, although it had its beginnings in 17th-century classicism, reveals a sensibility which is already almost Romantic.

Among the portrait painters must be remembered Duplessis, at his best in the portrait of Gluck, now in Vienna, and Boilly for his tiny paintings in the Musée Marmottan, and above all for his *Gohin Family* (Plate 8) where he has caught the typically self-satisfied and bourgeois atmosphere of a domestic environment on the eve of the Revolution, carefully depicting not only the people, but also the furniture and objects. It was left to Madame Vigée-Lebrun to bequeath an accurate and lifeless image of the aristocracy, which by this time was in a comatose state. Her paintings have a blend of languour and careless elegance which is both a little English and a little classical. They are more moving if one has read her later diaries, which are imbued with a constant nostalgic neurosis and full of regrets for a *douceur de vivre* lost for ever.

The work of Jacques Louis David accomplished the return to classicism that had been predicted by the critics, led by Diderot, and by the course of contemporary events. His *Oath of the Horatii*, painted in Rome in 1784, definitely marks the beginnings of the new trend in French painting, and had an unprecedented success in the following year's Salon. Even in Rome it had been not only curious onlookers who had crowded into David's studio in the Piazza del Popolo, but famous artists as well. Pompeo Batoni, who played quite an important role in the formation of Neo-classicism, Angelica Kauffmann, who was worshipped by everyone as the muse of the new movement, and Wilhelm Tischbein, Goethe's friend, were all united in a chorus of general enthusiasm for David. To understand the reasons for such immediate success one must remember that the *Horatii* not only admirably embodied the taste and ideas of the day, but also marked a renewal of the classicism that had been a constant feature of the arts in France since Poussin, interrupted only by Rococo. David conformed so well with the main stream of artistic tradition under Louis XVI that he only encountered approval and consent; but although he had perhaps always striven to achieve this, it was not always evident in his work. His first historical pictures, the *Battle of Mars and Minerva* (1770) or *Antiochus and Stratonice* (1774), clearly demonstrate his debt to Boucher and Fragonard (of whom at that time he might have seemed a disciple) and were only slightly affected by an attractive classicising tendency which his master Vien had passed on to him. Although the decorative colourful style is still predominant in *Antiochus and Stratonice* there are already indications of a leaning towards Poussinesque classicism. In *Belisarius asking for Alms* and *Andromache lamenting Hector* this 17th-century influence and the Neo-classical element are quite evident. David had obviously had time while in Rome to study not only the statuary of classical Greece and Rome but also the works of the Bolognese classicists, from Guido Reni to Domenichino. As Friedländer has remarked, he must have been able to examine Caravaggio's experiments in 'realism', as is evident in his *St Roch* (1779) now in Marseille.

The portraits he painted during the intervening years are among the highest achievements of the century in this field; the equestrian portrait of Count Potocki, which is almost a tribute to Rubens, would have been appreciated by painters of late Romanticism. The mischievous Louis XV-like sparkle of the portrait of Madame Pecoul belies an amazing accuracy of detail, from the lines of her face to her complicated laces and ribbons, reflecting a subtle psychological insight, tinged with good natured irony. It would take too long to examine in detail the art of David as a portrait painter, even if one only discussed the portraits painted during the reign of Louis XVI. The portrait of Marat, probably his highest achievement, and one of the most convincing portraits in the whole history of art, does not fall within the scope of this book. Nevertheless, the painting of the scientist Lavoisier, sitting at his desk with all the instruments of his profession before him, is painted with such amazing realism and pictorial force that it alone would disprove the accusation that David was a poor craftsman. The quality of the painting is very high in the *Horatii* as well, especially in the group of women, in spite of the yellowing of the colours. David was concerned with linking space in geometrical patterns in order to pinpoint and thereby emphasise the action. The small numbers of figures, another of his innovations, contributed to this effect. Evidently his interest was directed chiefly towards the values of drawing and composition, but this strictness of composition cannot disguise the beauty of the painting itself; it may not have the effervescence of Fragonard—all sparkling iridescence, delicate transparency and rosy flesh tints—but it has its own greatness. It is a different greatness but, as the saying goes, there is more than one path to Olympus. It is almost as though the many critics who were fascinated by Watteau and his followers became caught up in a romantic defence of the revolution those artists initiated (in a sense comparable to the similar developments of the Impressionists) and that they have thus ended up by denying, or refusing to recognise, the other aspect of 18th-century painting, led by David, which made

17. Jean Antoine Houdon (1741-1828).
Voltaire. 1780. Musée Fabre, Montpellier.

17. Jean Antoine Houdon (1741-1828). *Voltaire.* 1780. Musée Fabre, Montpellier. This plaster cast was taken by Houdon himself from the model for the famous marble given to the Comédie Française by the niece of the philosopher. Houdon put the finishing touches to this version of the sculpture, but not all the other replicas that exist are by the master's hand. They do prove, however, the importance given to this portrait which is one of the most successful of the century.

18. Louis Pierre Deseine (1749-1822). *The Dauphin (Louis XVII).* Versailles. The quality of the portrait bust is not exceptional, as the artist seems to have given greater importance to the detailed rendering of the lace collar than to the expression of the face, which as a result has no strength and shows little psychological insight. Apart from its historical interest the bust does have a certain elegance.

19. Jacques François Saly (1717-1776). *La Boudeuse.* Rijksmuseum, Amsterdam. Comparing this little portrait with the lifeless image of the son of Marie Antoinette in Plate 18 one can see how subtly and intelligently the artist has represented the capricious, pouting expression of the delightful child. Only Houdon could improve on this, as in the portraits of the Brongniart children, or in the figure of his own daughter Sabine.

18. Louis Pierre Deseine (1749-1822). *The Dauphin (Louis XVII).*

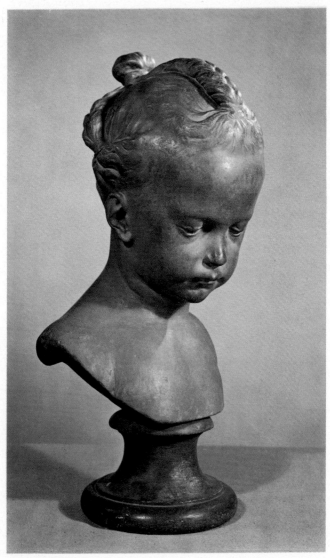

19. Jacques François Saly (1717-1776). *La Boudeuse.*
Rijksmuseum, Amsterdam.

an equal contribution to our artistic heritage. One can like Keats without disliking Browning.

After the resounding success of the *Horatii*, David's career continued in full sail with another painting where the composition is equally studied, *The Death of Socrates*, in which the artist wanted to prove himself as a master of expression. Reynolds, who was passing through Paris at the time, was perhaps exaggerating when he uttered the names Raphael and Michelangelo in the same breath as this work and declared it perfect in every way. In *Paris and Helen* (1788), illustrated in Plate 11, David seems to have paid an almost archaeological attention to every detail of the furniture and objects, and in *Brutus and his Dead Son*, painted the following year, this excessively scientific approach is carried to such extremes that the artistic merit suffers as a result. Brutus's head was drawn from the marble statue in the Campidoglio, those of the women from other Roman statues, and every single detail had its counterpart in classical art. Nevertheless the painting had enormous success, partly because of its moral undertones, to the extent that David became the symbol of the Revolution which was already under way, having started only a few weeks before the opening of the Salon in which *Brutus* was exhibited.

SCULPTURE

Many sculptors who started working in the Rococo style tried at a certain stage in their careers to come to some sort of compromise with classicism, or even to revise their ideas altogether; others were artists of transition who can be considered as protagonists of both styles. When the funeral monument of the Maréchal de Saxe was installed in the church of St Thomas at Strasbourg in 1777, it had been finished for several years, and the artistic life of the artist might have been considered over. Pigalle is usually thought of as a typically 'Pompadour' sculptor; but he was also one of the heralds of Neo-classicism, and this particular work shows a marked interest in the nobility of classical art. His nude *Voltaire,* sculpted between 1770 and 1776, made the philosopher himself exclaim: 'And some connoisseurs consider you old-fashioned!'

The case of Falconet is even stranger, for although he wanted to draw closer to the new artistic criteria his attachment was to Rococo, and even when he tried to be 'classical' a certain grace and delicacy betrayed an unintentional hedonism redolent of the reign of Louis XV. However, his contemporaries often considered his work absolutely classical, and Diderot went as far as to compare him, somewhat optimistically, to Phidias. Falconet himself cannot have been so convinced of the absolute supremacy of classical art, for in one of the rather controversial booklets he published occasionally he specifically says that though classical sculpture has a feeling for beauty it lacks the spark of life. J. J. Caffieri, of the famous family of bronze workers, lingered on delightfully in the tradition of Lemoyne, copying, although that is not the right word, his master's most fashionable busts, giving them an occasional flicker of truth beneath the surface and a wealth of verve and grace.

Under Louis XVI official commissions were nowhere near as numerous as they had been in the previous reign, to the extent that many sculptors were forced to look for work abroad, thus contributing indirectly to a wider diffusion of French art. Saly, for example, spent many years in Denmark, leaving there among other things a charming little portrait *La Boudeuse,* unexpectedly fresh and lifelike from the artist of the conventional *Faun with a Goat,* now in the Musée Cognacq-Jay. Caffieri ventured as far as Naples in the hope of obtaining a commission at Caserta, and the greatest French sculptor of the century, Houdon, crossed the Atlantic.

The relative scarcity of commissions also meant that sculptors almost always had to relinquish all thoughts of large scale monuments and concentrate on more modest works, small enough to be put in private palaces and apartments. Portraits were particularly suitable and gave plenty of scope for expressing a typically French, very rational, spirit of observation. This can be seen in the portraits by Augustin Pajou—that of Madame du Barry, for example, and even more in the noble human terracotta bust of the painter Hubert Robert. Pajou's work is considered by many people to be a point of contact between Pigalle and Houdon. He played a decisive part in defining the new style by collaborating with the architect Gabriel on the sculpture for the Opéra at Versailles, and he designed an enchanting green, blue, gold and silver interior for it. He directed a whole fleet of decorators who embellished it lavishly with sculpture in wood, plaster and stone and created one of the most successful ensembles of the period, which recent restoration revealed when a layer of banal 19th-century decoration was removed. Pajou was at his most Neo-classical in the allegorical group projected to commemorate the birth of the Dauphin. There are only a few small biscuit models of this and a terracotta model (recently brought to Versailles) as the group was never executed in marble because the Queen was offended by its nudity. This is a pity because it is one of the outstanding creations of the day, with its elegantly intertwined naked figures of Venus and the little Cupid (Marie Antoinette and the young heir) with the symbolic dolphin. However, the marble of *Psyche Abandoned* still exists; it was commissioned in 1785 as the pendant to a statue by Bouchardon. Even though prudery prevented this work being exhibited in the Salon it was such a success that the public used to go to see it in the artist's studio. By then, in 1791, times were changing, and he was able to sign it *'Citoyen de Paris'* instead of *'Sculpteur du Roi'*. The delicate curving lines of the body and the facial features, full of grief and charm, have prompted many art historians to regard *Psyche* as a predecessor to the work of Canova. This is surprising as it in no way approaches the impassive world of the genius from Possagno, who anyway by that time had already clearly established the principles of his art with his *Theseus and the Minotaur* and the funerary monument

20. Jean Antoine Houdon (1741-1828). *Winter.* 1783. Musée Fabre, Montpellier.

20. Jean Antoine Houdon (1741-1828). *Winter.* 1783. Musée Fabre, Montpellier. Commissioned by the financier Saint-Waast, this work caused a sensation in the Salon because of its semi-nudity. It is one of the major works of European art, not only for the extraordinary quality of the modelling but also for the originality of the concept. It has a pendant figure, *Summer*, sculpted two years later and conceived as a maiden crowned with flowers and with a sheaf of corn in her hands.

21. Augustin Pajou (1730-1809). *Portrait of a Young Woman.* Musée Jacquemart-André, Paris. The technical perfection of this charming terracotta bust is equalled by its gracefulness—these are the two qualities which are characteristic of all Pajou's work. With Falconet, Houdon and Pigalle he was one of the greatest modellers of the 18th century, having blended his particular delicate sentimentality with the restrained formalism of the day.

22. Claude Michel Clodion (1738-1814). Terracotta vase. Musée Cognacq-Jay, Paris. This is a delightful example of the Louis XVI side of Clodion's work. The decorations which adorn the vase, in the classicising style of the period, are all typical classical forms—fluting, ovolos and key patterns. The Rococo nature of the artist is shown by the twirls of roses in the garland.

21. Augustin Pajou (1730-1809). *Portrait of a Young Woman.*

of Clement XIV, where the feelings are carefully veiled in an irreproachable abstraction.

Pierre Julien began his career by collaborating with his master Guillaume Coustou the Younger on the huge cold construction that the latter erected in Sens cathedral as a tomb for the Dauphin, Louis XVI's father. Soon, however, he demonstrated his own ability in the *Dying Gladiator,* an elegant counterpart to the *Dying Gaul* in the Campidoglio, which won him entrance to the Academy in 1779. In 1787 he completed the *Nymph with the Goat Amaltea* for the royal dairy at Rambouillet. The interesting pyramidal composition, the frontal stance, the face in profile and the fluid gesture of her arm almost concealing her breast have a chillingly vibrant effect and reflect an accurate study of classical art. In his portrait of La Fontaine on the other hand Julien captured remarkably successfully the wise, ironic character of the writer. This statue is one of a series inspired by the ideas of Rousseau, and intended to honour great Frenchmen of all periods and at the same time to compensate to a certain extent for the relative lack of official commissions. Louis XVI's superintendent, the Comte d'Angiviller, who initiated the idea, approached the greatest sculptors of the day, and from 1776 to 1789 four statues were exhibited in every Salon. In this way Caffieri, Bernier, Clodion, Gois, Moitte, Boizot, Muchy, Julien and Pajou found a new means of subsistence and bequeathed to the nation their idealised monuments (often rather conventional and rhetorical) of the great men of the past.

22. Claude Michel Clodion (1738-1814). Terracotta vase. Musée Cognacq-Jay, Paris.

Clodion was an artist who, like Janus, faced in two directions at once: on the one side he turned to Rococo, which was his truest form of expression, even if more fanciful, and on the other he turned to classicism. But these two aspects of his art existed at the same time, so that beside drunken Bacchantes, caught in a moment of frenzied action there were chaste vestals of absolute purity of line. Side by side with his curly curving puppy there were the thoughtfully serious portrait of Montesquieu and the strictly formal decorative vases like the one in Plate 22. In this the echoes of classical Greece do not preclude rose garlands blooming in delicate symmetry.

Jean Antoine Houdon was the true 'lone wolf' of sculpture of the late 18th century and also of the early 19th century because his untiring activity continued even under the Empire. As a young man he stayed in Italy doing research which bordered on the scientific; he reminds one rather of Leonardo. In fact he diligently attended lectures in the dissection theatre. He writes of this himself with the significant words, 'I spent those years studying anatomy, which is the basis of design'. The effect was soon seen in his famous *Ecorché* of which countless copies and versions have been made, serving as models for art schools all over the world, and in the huge statues of *St John the Baptist* and *St Bruno,* commissioned for the church of Sta Maria degli Angeli. The former, which was only cast in plaster, fell to pieces at the end of the last century, so one can only admire the powerful gesture of the saint in the model in the Galleria Borghese, his arm extended in front of him, with the same severity as the *Ecorché*. St Bruno, however, is still *in situ*, and as Clement XIV said when he went to see it, 'He would talk if silence was not a rule of his order'.

Houdon's reputation was soon universal; he went to America to do a portrait of George Washington, but had to be content to show him standing rather than on horseback as he had hoped. (The comparison with Falconet's *Peter I on Horseback* would have been most enlightening.) Through Grimm he sent Catherine the Great of Russia a splendid marble of the *Huntress Diana,* which was sold by the Hermitage about thirty years ago and today is at the Gulbenkian Foundation in Lisbon. He made a bronze version of the same statue for the Duke of Gotha. Commissions from the court were, on the other hand, almost non-existent. He did a portrait of Louis XVI, but it was commissioned by the Paris Stockbrokers and depicted the monarch in such a dull and non-regal fashion that he was probably not encouraged to offer Houdon any further work, preferring to ask the distracted and casual Deseine to do the rather dapper portrait of the Dauphin. In compensation collectors commissioned various 'imaginative' works from him: for a financier he produced one of his masterpieces, *Winter,* seen as a young woman clutching her scanty shawl round her. For Madame Denis, Voltaire's niece, he executed the remarkable statue of the philosopher now in the foyer of the Comédie Française (Plate 17), an extraordinary combination of the demands of a portrait and pure idealisation. Above all there were his portrait busts: great men, charlatans, bourgeois, almost all the society of the day posed for him, were subjected to facial masks (like the one which nearly suffocated Washington), were measured, calculated, whether alive or dead, and were then recreated, injected with new blood and idealised—in a word they were reborn. Houdon's obsession for truth went so far that the corpse of Paul Jones, founder of the American Navy, has been identified thanks to the exactness of the measurements taken by Houdon. 'Preserving the reality of forms is the highest and most difficult aim for a sculptor' was the axiom to which the master remained loyal. Indeed few children more 'real' than the bust of his daughter Sabine or than the Brongniart children have ever been seen. Whether this is due to his measurements or his frequent visits to corpses remains uncertain.

There is something in Houdon's art which does not give the impression that he was a true representative of Neo-classicism. If one compares him to Canova, one can understand why. There is an involvement in his work which is too explicit, a subjective presence, here critical and ironical, there sentimentally emotional, and this goes beyond the discipline of his day to associate on the one hand with the Baroque, and on the other with Romanticism. If one looks closely at the threatening look of *Cagliostro,* the contemptuous expression of *Mirabeau,* the sour and haughty disillusion in the features of *Madame Adelaïde,* one seems to be more in the realm of personal interpretation than in that of impartial narration, despite the consciencious use of the ruler and compass. The same thing happened to Leonardo: sometimes the paths of science lead to the heights of individuality.

ARCHITECTURE

J. A. Gabriel, first architect to Louis XV, was completely inactive during the reign of Louis XVI (he lived until 1782), but it was with his later work that the real rethinking of the architectural orders of antiquity began. His Petit Trianon, that inimitable *folie* which was one of Louis XV's last gifts to Madame de Pompadour, was completed in 1764. In it there were already indications of a classical revival even though it was still very French in style; this was a classicism which could only have been created in the France of that time. Despite its modest size the building is most impressive, with the garden façade of four noble Corinthian columns rising above two flights of steps leading to the colourful flowerbeds. Gabriel was also the architect of the Opéra at Versailles, built in honour of the marriage of the future Louis XVI to Marie Antoinette in 1770. The room is a marvellous blend of the calm solemnity typical of the new era with the lighter sensitivity of previous years.

J. G. Soufflot had accompanied the Marquis de Marigny on his famous Italian tour in 1750 which many considered to have heralded the new style. In his church of Ste Geneviève, now known as the Panthéon, he appears as one of the initiators of Neo-classicism. The architect declared that he wanted

23. Jacques Ange Gabriel (1698-1782). The garden front of the Petit Trianon. 1762-1764. Versailles.

23.   Jacques Ange Gabriel (1698-1782). The garden front of the Petit Trianon. 1762-1764. Versailles. Although built as a *folie,* or little summer château, for Madame de Pompadour as a present from Louis XV, the Petit Trianon was entirely Neo-classical in style. All four façades are different; the one shown, which looks on to the gardens, is without doubt the richest, decorated with four imposing Corinthian columns, surmounted by an elegant balustrade.

24.   François Joseph Bélanger (1745-1818). The *folie at* Bagatelle. 1777. Built in a few weeks for the Comte d'Artois, the future Charles X, and a central influence for the new style, Bagatelle resembles the Petit Trianon by Gabriel in more than one way. This view shows the main façade in the distance on the left, essentially classical in line, with only a small porch for decoration. On the right is the little garden pavilion.

25.   Richard Mique (1728-1794). The Temple of Love. 1778. Versailles. Mique had been educated at Strasbourg, and then by Blondel in Paris. He became Marie Antoinette's favourite architect, and was entrusted by her with the making of her English gardens, designed by the painter Hubert Robert. This little temple is situated in the gardens of the Petit Trianon and is proof of the fashion for mythology of the late 18th century.

26.   Richard Mique (1728-1794). The Hamlet. Versailles. 'The fascination of a garden', declared Carmontelle, 'lies in being able to contemplate different vistas at every step.' Such a remark, and the fashion for 'nature' provoked by avid reading of Rousseau's novels, explain the appearance of buildings like this, which although picturesque still seem ingenuously ridiculous.

24. François Joseph Bélanger. (1745-1818). The *folie* at Bagatelle. 1777.

25. Richard Mique (1728-1794). The Temple of Love. 1778. Versailles.

26. Richard Mique (1728-1794). The Hamlet. Versailles.

to unite in this temple the lightness of Gothic buildings and the majesty of Greek architecture. In fact there are many Italian elements, from Bramante to Michelangelo, as Réau observed, combined with the whole Roman repertory, drawn particularly from the Pantheon of Agrippa, and needless to say there is nothing Gothic about it. The building, in the form of a Greek cross, is surmounted by an enormous dome ringed by thirty-two columns. The people who criticise its cold severity are often unaware that it was considerably altered and 'frozen' during the Revolution when, on the advice of Quatremère de Quincy at least forty-two windows were blocked up, and the bas-reliefs by Coustou and Houdon and much of the ornamentation were removed. At that time they were held to be useless puerilities.

The man who best knew how to create an entirely new architectural concept was C. N. Ledoux, who was already active during the last years of Louis XV's reign. He was the architect responsible for the residences built for Mademoiselle Guimard, the famous dancer whose portrait was painted by Fragonard, and for Mademoiselle Saint-Germain. The château at Benouville where he gave free reign to his love for the grandiose brought financial ruin to the Marquis de Livry. The key work of those years was the pavilion at Louveciennes which Ledoux built for Madame du Barry between 1770 and 1771 and which was to become the example of the Louis XVI style *par excellence,* and a treasure house of the most beautiful *objets d'art* of the day which are now dispersed in museums all over the world. The genius of Ledoux is most apparent in the impressive town plan for Arc-et-Senans with the Chaux salt works. He designed a town of circular plan in which all the buildings were classical in style and of obvious didactic and moral implications. There were a Temple to Memory, a House of Instruction, Public Baths and even a House of Pleasure with a phallus-shaped ground plan, where according to Ledoux the demonstration of vice would encourage sinners to return to the straight and narrow. Unfortunately this extraordinary urban programme, which makes one think *mutatis mutandis* of certain contemporary concepts, was never realised as a whole, and what was built was partly destroyed by revolutionaries.

The same fate befell some of the creations of another unusual architect, E. L. Boullée, who conceived a law courts raised above a prison, thus offering the magnificent spectacle of vices being crushed beneath the weight of justice. Another project of his, for Newton's cenotaph, planned as an enormous sphere surrounded by several rings of cypress trees, is disturbingly modern. 'Our buildings ought to be like poems,' are words which might have been spoken by Frank Lloyd Wright. But Boullée's ideas seldom got any further than the paper they were drawn on, and it is a pity that these Utopian freemason concepts were not translated into ideal stage sets for Mozart's *Magic Flute*, for they seem to have the same sense of magic reasoning. On the whole Ledoux was more fortunate, because in 1783 he was able to build the new city walls of Paris and the forty-seven little pavilions of the toll houses, which he took an emphatic delight in baptising *propilaea*. Only four of them are still standing but the others can be studied from the architect's drawings. They are magnificent exercises on the themes of classical architecture, some inspired by the Doric temples of Paestum, others by domed rotunda or, like the one still *in situ* at La Villette, by the Pantheon.

Victor Louis worked to begin with under the patronage of Madame Geoffrin, 'the Queen Mother of Poland' as she was maliciously called, who introduced him to Stanislas Poniatowski. Louis owes his fame to the colonnades of the Palais Royal in Paris, which frame the gardens with their beautiful proportions, evoking the Palladian atmosphere of Venice and Vicenza. Palladio also appears to have inspired the designs for the façade of the theatre at Bordeaux, to which Louis gave a splendid Corinthian colonnade surmounted by statues. This makes a fitting entrance to the impressive foyer dominated by a majestic stairway leading to peristyles on the first floor. A hundred years later Charles Garnier was to make full use of this architectural device in the Paris Opéra.

It would be impossible to discuss all the architects who distinguished themselves in one way or another in the late 18th century, much less to examine individual works, but it would not be right to leave out the Ecole de Médecine by Gondoin, which Quatremère de Quincy considered the greatest building of the entire century. Even if one does not share this opinion, one cannot deny the originality of Gondoin's concept. Either side of the entrance portal extends a double portico of Ionic columns between which are wrought iron grilles; the whole is surmounted by an Attic storey with an allegorical bas-relief in the centre. Between the columns one glimpses the great court, and on the far side the dissection theatre, crowned by a powerful sculpted pediment.

Among public buildings the most notable was the Hôtel des Monnaies by Antoine and, among religious edifices, the church of St Philippe du Roule by Chalgrin and the Capuchin convent on the Chaussée d'Antin by Brongniart. An admirable example of a private dwelling and one of the highlights of Parisian architecture is the Hôtel de Salm, which Pierre Rousseau completed in 1789, with one façade on the Seine and the other on the rue de Lille, in the manner of a triumphal arch. After later additions and reconstructions it became the headquarters of the Légion d'Honneur. The *folie* of Bagatelle was built by Bélanger in two months for the Comte d'Artois, who thus won his bet with Marie Antoinette. It is one of the most exquisite examples of a small suburban residence, as well as being a tribute to the art of the creator of Neo-classicism, Gabriel, whose Petit Trianon is emulated in the elegant, beautifully proportioned façade and the exquisite finish of every detail.

SILVERWARE AND OBJETS D'ART

The famous *Supplique* of 1754, in which among other things Cochin exhorted goldsmiths to straighten the stems of candelabra and to stop making everyone

27. Jacques Nicolas Roettiers (active 1765-1777). Silver
water cooler. Musée Nissim de Camondo, Paris.

28. Gabriel Gerbu. Silver candelabra.

27. Jacques Nicolas Roettiers (active 1765-1777). Silver water cooler. Musée Nissim de Camondo, Paris. The work of Jacques Nicolas Roettiers is outstanding among 18th-century French silver. This water cooler is a piece from the service that Catherine the Great of Russia gave to her favourite Orloff, and was made between 1770 and 1771. It has all the characteristics of the Louis XVI style as well as perfection of execution which is especially evident in the garland of ivy leaves.

28. Gabriel Gerbu (active during the last quarter of the 18th century). Silver candelabra. Musée des Arts Decoratifs, Paris. Even among less ambitious silverware there were objects of a pleasingly elegant line and they were always accurately made. The decorative motifs are copied from designs by the more famous decorators, in this case Delafosse, who was particularly fond of cascades of garlands.

29. Louis XVI andiron. Louvre, Paris. Bronzework reached its apogee in this period. The linear composition of this magnificent object, the elegant balance and perfect execution make it an outstandingly satisfying piece. The detail is particularly noteworthy, like the drapery swathed from the lion's haunch to the plinth, forming a graceful link.

30. Louis XVI clock. Petit Palais, Paris. The circular movement of this clock was not infrequently found in the late 18th century. The two dials, or bands of numbers, move round while the tongue of the upturned serpent marks the hour. The clock is the work of one of the Lepaute family—probably Jean Baptiste—who were active in Paris for more than two centuries.

29. Louis XVI andiron. Louvre, Paris.

30. Louis XVI clock. Petit Palais, Paris.

giddy with the excessive contortions of Rococo, passed unheeded for a long time, even though Meissonier, one of the greatest champions of Rococo, had died as early as 1750. Goldsmiths were slow to follow fashion and the same models were repeated in one studio for so long that objects in pure Louis XV style were still being manufactured when the century drew to its close. The influence of Thomas Germain, the greatest artist of the century in this field, lasted for many years. The shapes he evolved were never excessively twisted and always had an unobtrusive elegance; they were still being reproduced after the appearance of Neo-classical models.

The relative scarceness of silver in the 18th century is partly explained by continual meltings-down, enforced by the state of the economy, by changing fashions and by various new laws. In the second half of the century the appearance of new alloys and the growing diffusion of plated objects within reach of a wide clientèle indicated a changed social and economic situation. The use of porcelain or of certain white faience, which was now quite common, was detrimental to the spread of silver. Yet about 1750 there were no less than five hundred goldsmiths' workshops in Paris, many of which also served foreign customers. In order to date silver, at least the silver made in Paris, one only has to refer to a handbook, to check the marks or punches with which it was always stamped, thus establishing the chronology as exactly as one can with English silver.

In the 1770s the plant forms of Rococo began to be replaced by a weird new menagerie—sphinxes, griffons and lions—together with ornamental motifs taken from classical temples. The straight line triumphed, embellished with fine beading, fluting, ribbon motifs and laurel leaves, giving a solemn dignity to the miniature monuments made to adorn dining tables. The father of 18th-century goldsmiths, Thomas Germain, had had other pupils besides his son François Thomas, among whom was R. J. Auguste. François Thomas's activity ended with the sensational bankruptcy of 1765; most of his works were direct imitations of his father's models and fell strictly within the limits of Rococo. Auguste on the other hand was one of the first to show a lively interest in the new Neo-classical forms. He made his shapes as simple as possible, and at times they look as though they were copied from classical bas-reliefs. Among his most successful works were the terrines presented by Count Creutz to Gustavus III of Sweden in 1774. They were decorated with allegories in relief in honour of the sovereign, after models attributed to the sculptor Pajou. There was also a large, very elegant soup tureen, dated 1789, formerly in the Puiforcat collection. The base is supported by four one-footed winged lions, a motif which was to be extremely successful under the Empire. On this rests the bowl, almost kylix shaped, with beautiful handles set in classical masks, and decorated with a frieze of acanthus leaves. A statuette representing virtue bearing a laurel wreath crowns the lid.

Apart from Gerbu, who usually followed the elegant if somewhat repetitive designs of Delafosse, and Bréant, who always produced objects of excellent quality and pleasing line, and Cheret, Modenx, Bonhomme and Boullier, there was of course J. N. Roettiers. Instructed in the art by his father, who was a disciple of Meissonnier, the great arbiter of Rococo, he was nevertheless one of the first to turn to account the new classicising pattern books. Together with Auguste he became the most famous and most sought after Parisian goldsmith of the Louis XVI period. This is proved by the many important commissions he was given. It was Roettiers who made the important service of more than a thousand pieces that Catherine the Great gave to her favourite Gregory Orloff, and then bought back again complete when the prince died in 1783. The service is now split up in different collections; the pieces in the Musée Nissim de Camondo, all dated 1770-1771, are not only examples of consummate technical skill but show a marked feeling for modelling and are of a strong, elegant shape (Plate 27). Unfortunately, apart from these exquisitely made works, the general run of Louis XVI silverware was often of a much lower standard. Increasing mass production, especially of the smaller pieces, involved the manufacture of simple pierced and cut-out bands, which held blue glass containers for salt, oil etc. Many second rate goldsmiths used to mount their works with the help of screws, rather than soldering them. This was really the dividing line between art and industry, although for a while the two existed side by side even under the Empire.

Among the first to show an interest in the spirit of the new classicism in bronze-working, Philippe

Caffieri is particularly notable; he was the son of Jacques, the greatest bronze worker under Louis XV. Not many of his works still exist, except for the railings of the stairway of the Palais Royal, and most of them are ecclesiastical. The candelabra of Bayeux cathedral are particularly important, as are the Pascal candelsticks at Clermont Ferrand, signed and dated 1771. The latter already have all the familiar Louis XVI features: tripod form, garlands of leaves and flowers, draped ribands and lions' paws. Pierre Gouthière was one of the most gifted bronze-workers of all time, raising his art to the level of genius. The exquisite finish of the objects which passed through his hands is so outstanding that any high quality French bronze, which, as often happens, is not marked with the maker's name, will usually be attributed to him. For example, for years the bronze decoration of Riesener's furniture has been thought to be his work, which is in fact most improbable. The only bronze known to date which bears Gouthière's signature is the clock presented to a member of the Rochechouart family by the city of Avignon in 1771; but many others can be attributed to him, either from old documents or catalogues or, less certainly, from the way each piece is made. The task of the chaser was to hand finish the rough-cast bronze objects by chiselling the surface with various implements. It is particularly this finishing, and the special matt gilding which he invented, which makes the light shine on all the little facets as if it were pure gold, that distinguishes the unrivalled skill of Gouthière.

The court, or more particularly the family, of

31. Pierre Gouthière (1732-1813/14). Serpentine vase
mounted in gilt bronze. Louvre, Paris

32. Louis XVI gilt bronze sconce. Musée des Arts
Décoratifs, Paris.

Louis XVI was neither as aware nor as sensitive to the really important innovations as it had been previously, and consequently it did not use its wealth to advantage. It was left to certain nobles to take an interest in Gouthière, among whom were the Duchesse de Mazarin, the Duc d'Aumont, and Madame du Barry. The latter commissioned him to make innumerable objects for her pavilion at Louveciennes, and these most expensive trinkets may have been one of the causes of her ruin. In 1793, shortly before she died on the scaffold, she still owed him the astronomical sum of 750,000 libres.

The Duc d'Aumont had an absolute passion for semi-precious stones and anything in marble or breccia. He was very probably one of the first to take advantage of the talent of the young Gouthière, entrusting him with a number of his precious objects, which are interesting today more for their extraordinary bronze mounts than for anything else. Many of these are preserved in the Wallace Collection in London, and in the Louvre. Plate 31 shows an example of his skill—a serpentine vase which appeared in the catalogue of the sale of the Duke's possessions shortly after his death in 1782, and which was bought by Marie Antoinette. The vase stands on a base consisting of a truncated column, opening out into a cup-shape, only to curve in gently higher up. Here the chaser has carved the exquisite figures of a naiad and a faun, the garlands they bear repeating the bronze decoration. Other motifs decorate the middle of the vase and the edge of the cover, which is crowned by a minute bronze bunch of grapes.

Beside the splendid genius of Gouthière shine many stars of less intensity, who nevertheless were responsible for works which set the tone for craftsmanship all over Europe. Feuchère, for example, made the sconces commissioned by the Queen in 1788 for her *cabinet de toilette* at St Cloud. These delightful pieces have three branches, rotating from a support which is adorned with a pair of turtle doves on top. The central arm is in the guise of a Cupid carrying a flaming heart in his hand, while the other two are myrtle branches, crowned with fruit and decorated with gadrooning.

There are many more objects of high quality which, as they are not signed, must remain anonymous. Among these are the beautiful sconces in the Musée des Arts Décoratifs, which seem to celebrate the myth of Daphne with the caryatids half transformed into trees (Plate 32). Then there are the marvellous andirons in the Louvre, shaped like classical vases, which rise in a wealth of garlands and shells from a cubical base. This base is embellished in its turn with a bas-relief of a pair of cherubs, who are joined by sumptuous drapery, like a chariot, to the nearby winged lion, roaring at the mysterious splendour of the flames.

TAPESTRIES, TEXTILES AND WALLPAPER

The Beauvais and Gobelins factories do not have any particular interest as far as the development

31.   Pierre Gouthière (1732-1813/4). Serpentine vase mounted in gilt bronze. Louvre, Paris. This superb *objet d'art* belonged to Marie Antoinette who bought it at the Duc d'Aumont's sale in 1782. The great collector had commissioned it directly from Gouthière, whom he patronised and for whom he had procured an important clientèle, including the Duchesse de Mazarin, the Comte d'Artois and Madame du Barry.

32.   Louis XVI gilt bronze sconce. Musée des Arts Décoratifs, Paris. An unbridled imagination reigned during this period in top French workshops. Sconces were a pretext for all sorts of exercises. The curving abstract shapes of Rococo were abandoned for serpents, hunting horns (like those made for the Queen at the Petit Trianon) or exquisite mythological themes.

33.   *The Watering Place.* From the series 'Country Pastimes'. Beauvais tapestry. 1772-1779. Mobilier National, Paris. Late 18th-century tapestry is relatively only moderately interesting because of the intervention of the directors of the factories, like Le Brun and Oudry, which was in a sense negative, as they enforced the direct copying of painters' cartoons. Among the most beautiful tapestries of the time is the one illustrated, which is from a series designed by Francesco Casanova.

34.   Silk from the Lyon workshop. Musée des Tissus, Lyon. The man who made this fabric, Philippe de La Salle, played a decisive role in the development of Lyon textiles and in their success at this time. Here he has depicted a Russian eagle hovering victorious over the Turkish arms, in compliance with the wishes of Catherine the Great who commissioned the silk.

33. *The Watering Place.* From the series 'Country Pastimes'.
Beauvais tapestry. 1772-1779. Mobilier National, Paris.

of the Louis XVI style is concerned. They continued more than anything else to repeat the series of tapestries which were most successful under the previous reign, and what was created had little originality. Under the direction of Oudry there had been a tendency to follow as faithfully as possible the cartoons of the painter, which gave the weavers no freedom at all, and this was now carried to the extreme. Very occasionally in the past small pictures in wool had been woven at the Gobelins, and now the production of these tapestry-pictures was quite considerable. They were really almost *trompe-l'œil,* for although they stirred the imagination and gratified a taste for the bizarre they can hardly be called tapestries. Portraits of royalty and the most popular compositions of Greuze, van Loo and even of Rembrandt were reproduced in this way, in wool and silk, framed like genuine paintings, and hung on the wall among all the other pictures, as can be seen in the miniature on the famous snuffbox of the Duc de Choiseul. The series of large tapestries on the *Habits and Customs of the East,* designed by A. van Loo between 1772 and 1776, were basically copied from Louis XV prototypes. In Callet's *Seasons,* however, the classical world makes its appearance, with the usual device of the Roman banquet with the three-legged stools, altars and togas. The *History of Henry IV* is a result of the commemorative spirit which inspired, at the same period, the series of statues of great Frenchmen, while the *History of France* cycle, with its ambitious allegorical, didactic purpose has something in common with some 19th-century

34. Silk from the Lyon workshop. Musée des Tissus, Lyon.

painting, or even with the colossal epics of the screen of our time, like those of Cecil B. De Mille. Among the many subjects are *The Death of Leonardo da Vinci* and the *Assassination of Coligny*.

The Louis XVI style is better expressed in certain materials than in the tapestries, particularly in silks from Lyon and in the *toiles de Jouy*. One great artist from Lyon, Philippe de la Salle, was responsible for some of the gayest and most elegant textiles of the time. He had, as few others have had, a really intelligent feeling for his material, and made full use of the decorative possibilities of silk. There is a delightful poetry in his bouquets of ferns, anemones and roses, in the eagle hovering over simulated drapes and peacock feathers, in the priestess adorning an altar with garlands beneath an arbour of flowering myrtle, and there is only a gentle nostalgia for the classical world with no trace of academicism. From the technical point of view he managed to achieve three shades of every colour, which allowed unusual subtleties of light and relief. Gaspard Grégoire, another talented craftsman who worked in Lyon, deserves to be remembered here for his figured velvets. Until 1759 there had been a prohibition on the manufacture of printed fabrics in France, but from that year they were produced at Mulhouse and above all at Jouy where the German Oberkampf profited from the advice of the painter-decorator, J. B. Huet. Initially the designs were on a white background, sometimes imitating those on Indian and Persian textiles, sometimes *chinoiseries* in Rococo style. Later, stripes appeared, and also cameos,

35. Large Sèvres vase. 1783. Louvre, Paris.

35.   Large Sèvres vase. 1783. Louvre, Paris. Towards the end of the monarchy, the Sèvres factory tended to produce large, absolutely perfectly made pieces. The example illustrated is more than six feet high, and is made of biscuit panels modelled by Boizot and bronzes minutely chased by Thomire.

36.   Sèvres porcelain vase mounted in gilt bronze. Louvre, Paris. The fashion for porcelain mounted in bronze lasted during the reign of Louis XVI, although the Rococo mounts of the first half of the century gave way to the simpler forms inspired by antiquity. When porcelain of a single colour was used as a foil to the bronze, the result is particularly striking.

37.   Cup and teapot in *porcelaine de Paris.* Made in the workshop of the Duc d'Orléans. Louvre, Paris. Gradually factories other than Sèvres were allowed to produce porcelain, thus removing the monopoly that Sèvres had had until then, and various factories sprang up in Paris under the protection of the highest nobles at court. The Queen's workshop was in the rue Thiroux and adopted a crowned 'A' in blue or pink as its mark.

36. Sèvres porcelain vase mounted in gilt bronze.

37. Cup and teapot in *porcelaine de Paris*. Made in the
workshop of the Duc d'Orléans. Louvre, Paris.

garlands and little scenes, either *à la grecque* or pastoral; in some cases they were scenes from romantic tales, like *Paul et Virginie,* or allegorical subjects.

J. B. Reveillon must be mentioned here for the important rôle he played in the manufacture of *papier peint,* or wallpaper, during this period. He availed himself of the collaboration of painter-decorators such as Pillement, Cietti, Lavallée, Poussin and Boucher the younger, as well as Huet, all of whom provided designs. These wallpapers were not only used to cover the walls of many houses with their gay patterns, instead of very expensive brocades, but, keeping up with the latest fashions, were found everywhere, even on Montgolfier's balloon, which was made of these same wallpapers by Reveillon. Needless to say, the favourite motifs employed by the factory were the usual Louis XVI themes— pastoral scenes, arabesques inspired by the decorations at Herculaneum and Pompeii and mythological subjects.

PORCELAIN

In the late 18th century the Sèvres factory took the lead almost entirely in the production of porcelain in Europe, even if it rarely achieved the same amazing level of innovation it had had under Louis XV. However where the production of the factory lost some of its creative originality, its fantasy and grace, it gained in quality, for the manufacture had never reached such perfection.

This is not to say that new shapes and motifs did not produce objects of great beauty, but it is fair to say that when Falconet's administration ended in 1766, and the sculptor left for St Petersburg, the most outstanding period in the history of Sèvres came to an end. L. S. Boizot succeeded him a few years later and carried on his work, often with very pleasing results, although under his direction Sèvres never recaptured the subtle grace of Falconet's models, which came halfway between the delicate sophistication of Rococo and the more literary world of Neoclassicism. When d'Angiviller became director of the factory, after the muddled years of Parent's administration, he exercised a profitable and judicious influence and made great efforts to inject it with more vitality by commissioning spectacular works like the vase made in 1783 after designs by Boizot (Plate 35). Apart from its remarkable size (it stood about six feet high) and its original colouring (bas-reliefs in biscuit and deep blue porcelain), it also boasted bronzes by Thomire, which among other things served to hide the joins between the different pieces. Other unusual pieces were made during those years at Sèvres, like the pair of vases called Mars and Minerva (only the latter still exists) where polychrome was discarded in order to give greater emphasis to the exquisite gilt bronze mounts.

The factory at Sèvres had many sides, often in direct contrast, so that although there were the usual signs of a classical style, objects in Rococo taste were still being made up to the last moments of the *ancien régime,* and these were not just copies of existing models. For example, there was the dark blue service started for Louis XVI in 1783 and still not finished at his death. It was made in soft paste porcelain despite the fact that the discovery of kaolin had permitted the manufacture of hard paste porcelain in France since 1770. There were also innumerable vases and ornaments still decorated with *chinoiseries* although they tended to be rather more freely interpreted. It was a long time before the Neo-classical style penetrated Sèvres, and then it was accepted only tentatively, which is understandable in an art which was passed from one craftsman to another, from father to son. The service made for Madame du Barry in 1770-1771 was still Rococo in design, although it was perhaps a somewhat constrained Rococo; but the decoration in particularly delicate colours has many classical motifs, like the enchanting garlands intertwined with little blue urns crowned with pink flowers.

The two medallions of Marie Antoinette and Louis XVI—or *Louis le Populaire,* as the inscription calls him with pathetic irony—were made in 1774 to commemorate the sovereign's ascent to the throne, and are now in the Niarchos Collection..These are an indication that Neo-classicism had finally crossed the threshold of Sèvres, and this is even more evident in the piece modelled in biscuit two years later by Boizot, where the two sovereigns join their right hands like Jupiter and Juno over a neo-Attic altar decorated with rams' heads and garlands.

Catherine the Great of Russia is well known to have had a passion for art and for French culture;

38. Reconstruction of a Louis XVI interior.

38. Reconstruction of a Louis XVI interior. Salle Lebaudy, Louvre, Paris. The *boiseries* and the mantlepiece come from the Luynes palace in Paris and date from about 1770. The large candelabrum in the background on the right, supported by a female figure, is the work of J. F. Lorta (1788). The chairs by Boulard come from the Château de Montreuil and still have their petit point upholstery embroidered by the King's sister, Madame Elisabeth, and her ladies.

39. Georges Jacob (1739-1814). Armchair. 1787. Louvre, Paris. Georges Jacob is probably the greatest French furniture-maker of the period, except for Riesener. This little armchair *de cabinet* rests on four bracket legs and is decorated with fluting and a fret.

40. Georges Jacob (1739-1814). Armchair. Musée Marmottan, Paris. A perfect example of the so-called 'Etruscan' style; the top crossbar of the back has a painted motif which was obviously taken from some 'Etruscan' vase, while the lower bar is pierced with palmettes. The arms rest on simplified animal forms, and the front legs are inspired by the findings of Italian archaeologists, those at the back being bow legs.

41. Reconstruction of a Louis XVI drawingroom. Musée Nissim de Camondo, Paris. Both the *boiseries* and the furniture of this room date from the last quarter of the century. The centre table has four legs and two marble shelves, and is placed in the middle of the room as its name implies; the top revolves for greater convenience. The large Aubusson carpet with a green background dates from about 1765 to 1775.

39. Georges Jacob (1739-1814). Armchair. 1787. Louvre, Paris.

40. Georges Jacob (1739-1814). Armchair. Musée Marmottan, Paris.

41. Reconstruction of a Louis XVI drawingroom. Musée
Nissim de Camondo, Paris.

she was one of the first supporters of Neo-classicism and it was she who commissioned from Sèvres the most beautiful dinner service of the period. It consisted of more than seven hundred pieces, which are now scattered in the greatest collections in the world. The decoration has Pompeii red medallions with monochrome motifs copied from classical cameos—profiles, nymphs chased by fauns, trophies —surrounded by richly gilt vine-trails; the white bands are threaded with garlands of flowers and the background is a beautiful turquoise blue. In the centre of every plate, standing out clearly from the white background, is the monogram of the Tsarina surmounted by an imperial crown. The delightfully luminous colours lend grace to the studied classical patterns. The service was delivered to Catherine in 1779. When the Comtesse du Nord, wife of the Grand Duke Paul, the son and heir of Catherine, visited Paris three years later she was presented by Marie Antoinette with the gift of a *service de toilette* in *porcelaine de France,* as it was then called, which is still in the Pavlovsk palace for which it was originally intended. It consisted of some seventy pieces (there was even a tongue scraper); some were mounted in gold by Duplessis and others were embellished with biscuit figures modelled in the round by Boizot, but they are all strongly classical in feeling. Some of the jugs and the powder box are almost exact copies of Greek vases, and very similar to some of the pieces created in the factory at Naples. (When four years later Louis XVI acquired the whole of Denon's collection of 'Etruscan' vases, he decided to deposit them at Sèvres so that their shapes and decoration would serve as models for the craftsmen.) Thus it was that perhaps the two most successful creations from the factory found their way to Russia.

Even at Sèvres, however, a certain foreign influence was welcome, and copies were produced of the beautiful white Wedgwood friezes on their blue background and on certain lacquer backgrounds typical of other factories. The business suffered a great setback when other centres were granted licences by royal decree for the manufacture of objects in porcelain. These various factories, which nearly always flourished under the lofty patronage of some member of the royal family—the Comte de Provence at Rue Clignancourt, at Limoges the Comte d'Artois, or the Queen herself in Paris—produced pieces of great beauty, inspired, it is true, by those of Sèvres, but capable of standing comparison with the products of the old and glorious factory.

FURNITURE

'How grateful I am to you: the magnificent table arrived in perfect condition ten days ago and everyone is admiring this marvellous piece of work.' So starts a letter, dated 4th March 1777, from the Empress of Austria, Maria Theresa, in Vienna to her daughter Marie Antoinette, Queen of France; and those opening lines are a significant indication of the passion for furniture nurtured in the 18th century. This is not an isolated case, as one gathers by glancing through the

42. Louis XVI style console. Musée Condé, Chantilly.

42.   Louis XVI style console. Musée Condé, Chantilly. This console, according to Pierre Verlet's findings, must be an excellent copy made in the last century of another identical console which was smaller and made in about 1780. This is proof of how difficult it can be to date a piece of furniture only from the stylistic point of view.

43.   Adam Weisweiler (b. *c.* 1750, active until 1809). Writing table. 1784. Louvre, Paris. This object, which is more like a jewel than a piece of furniture, was given to the Queen for the Château de St Cloud by Daguerre, the famous *marchand-mercier,* who was a very influential figure in the decorative arts of the Louis XVI period. It is decorated with bronzes attributed to Gouthière and with plaques of ebony and Chinese lacquers, one of which lifts up to form a book-rest.

44.   Reconstruction of a Louis XVI interior. Musée Carnavalet, Paris. This room from the Breteuil palace in Paris has been transferred exactly as it stands to the Musée Carnavalet. All the decorations are in Neo-classical style. The chair in the foreground is particularly interesting as the back echoes the shape of the Montgolfiers' balloon; it was at this time that the first flights in the balloon had been made in Paris.

43. Adam Weisweiler. Writing table. 1784.

44. Reconstruction of a Louis XVI interior. Musée Carnavalet, Paris.

letters of Stanislas Augustus Poniatowski, King of Poland, to Madame Geoffrin, or at the correspondence of Catherine the Great. The latter for instance wrote to her Parisian artistic advisor, the writer Grimm, on 26th November 1785 with these words: 'David Roentgen and his two hundred drawers have arrived safely and at just the right moment to satisfy my gluttony.' The famous German cabinet-maker, who had a workshop in Paris as well, had travelled all the way to St Petersburg to deliver to the Empress a piece of furniture made to hold her precious collection of carved gems. Catherine's heir and his consort, during their visit to Paris in 1782, had such unbridled enthusiasm for furniture that they were not content with visiting all the palaces and châteaux of the royal family, nor with the ritual pilgrimage to the *hôtel* of the Duc d'Aumont, which was one of leading shrines of the new style. They had to go to the workshops of the major cabinet-makers themselves and even ventured as far as the house of Mademoiselle Dervieux—the queen of the *demi-monde,* according to their escort the Baroness Ober-kirch—which they considered 'an enchanting choco-late-box'.

By this time the style which is nowadays called, perhaps improperly, Louis XVI, had already reached its apogee although, as far as furniture is concerned, its beginnings went back to the mid 1760s. Commodes *à la grecque* were even mentioned in Madame de Pompadour's will as early as 1764, and from then on Baron Grimm began his protestations against this infatuation for things Greek, which increased daily.

Naturally in the beginning it was only a question of tentative movements towards a greater strictness in decoration and in the lines of furniture, which in other ways retained many Rococo characteristics. Thus even when the upper part of a commode began to straighten out, the legs and sometimes the decoration would still be full of movement, reflecting a feminine style which had little to do with antiquity.

In a watercolour of 1771 by Moreau the Younger, depicting the ceremonial opening of the pavilion of Louveciennes, there are several chairs with straight legs and horseshoe-shaped backs which have been identified in Madame du Barry's receipts. They were executed by the cabinet-maker Delanois and were in Berlin until the second World War. The only one known today is in a private collection; it still has its beautiful gilding on a white background and its decoration of motifs drawn from the classical repertory. These early pieces have a freedom and grace which is not usually associated with the Louis XVI style; at that time the cabinet-makers were content to interpret the classical style without trying to simulate it. There is nothing pedantic about their furniture, no attempt to indicate a series of moral rules for everyday life; the only aim was to please with no pedantic undertones. Many elements were indeed taken entirely from classical monuments, or rather from engravings published by Caylus, and were adapted by the most fashionable decorators of the day, but they still have a distinctly 18th-century flavour typical of the image of the period which springs to mind. The only failing is an exaggerated fondness for decoration.

Never have bronzes been so rich, nor used in such profusion. Cascades of garlands, scattered ribbons, rose branches, hyacinths and flowers of all kinds spill over commode fronts, framing the motifs worked in inlay on the various compartments. Nor had the making of them ever reached such perfection. Very varied effects of light and colour were required for the various types of gilding, and the chiselling was nearly as fine as in goldsmith's work. The inlaid work was equally rich, using the pictorial possibilities of about sixty rare and exotic woods, which had been gradually added to the forty or more well known national species. When this was not enough to satisfy the demands for much prized polychromy they were tinted artificially, or mother-of-pearl was used, as in the incredible secrétaire which belonged to Marie Antoinette. It was decorated with steel as well as with gilt bronze mounts and, according to literary sources, others carried butterfly wings. Furniture with porcelain plaques, held in place by thin bronze frames, was given pride of place in the interiors at Louveciennes. Other plaques, in metal, worked by Gouthière for astronomical sums were presented for the adoration of the faithful by the Duc d'Aumont, who also had console tables made only from marble, and furniture entirely set with semi-precious stones.

In deference to the fashion for colour, chairs and divans, which, unlike commodes, were not in veneered wood, were painted in various colours, not always, as is the widespread belief, in pale unobtrusive shades. Strong contrasts were usually preferred which would be called excessive today, and

45. Bernard Molitor (*c.* 1730-after 1811). Secrétaire.
Louvre, Paris.

46. Jean Georges Schlichtig (*c.* 1725-1782). Commode.
Louvre, Paris.

45.   Bernard Molitor (*c.* 1730-after 1811). Secrétaire. Louvre, Paris. This fall-front secrétaire, decorated with lacquer panels and veneered with ebony, is one of a pair; a similar one is now in the British royal collections. It is so close to the style of Empire furniture (except for the lacquer panels) that Grandjean has recently suggested that it might be dated about 1820. On the other hand there are many who think it dates from the end of Louis XVI's reign.

46.   Jean Georges Schlichtig (*c.* 1725-1782). Commode. Louvre, Paris. This commode, which is still in transitional style, has Marie Antoinette's initials in mother-of-pearl on the corners. The inlays are also in mother-of-pearl and in ivory, depicting architectural views and people dressed in the fashion of the day. Works by this cabinet-maker are quite rare.

47.   Louis XVI fall-front secrétaire. Wallace Collection, London. This piece is almost oppressive in its opulent decoration, covered with gilt bronzes which, among other things, include two female heads at the corners and a large coat-of-arms above a lion's head on the front flap. The woods of the inlay are of different types (some of them are dyed): sycamore, purple-wood and rose-wood. The work has been attributed to Antoine Foulet.

48.   Louis XVI secrétaire. Private collection, Paris. This is a typical fall-front secrétaire; the top flap drops down to rest on the two doors of the lower half which conceal drawers. It is richly decorated with gilt bronzes (those on the corners are in the style of Delafosse) and is topped by a marble slab over a drawer which looks like a bronze frieze. The piece is attributed to the cabinet-maker Boudin (1735-1804).

47. Louis XVI fall-front secrétaire.

48. Louis XVI secrétaire. Private collection, Paris.

combinations like yellow and red were used (as, for example, in the drawingroom which exists in the museum of the Ca'Rezzonico in Venice). Lacquer panels were still used, both genuine oriental ones and European imitations (like the so-called *vernis Martin*), which, as has justly been observed, seem to be rather an anachronism on furniture intended to recreate the spirit of Greece and Rome. But it would be impossible to explain all the caprices of fashion. Furniture by the cabinet maker Boulle, for example, in a style which was poles apart from Louis XVI, was not only collected during this period, but even copied, on behalf of some of the leading advocates of the *retour à l'antique* like Lalive de Jully. On the other hand the triumph of Neo-classicism did not inhibit the manufacture of pieces in pure Rococo style; on the contrary, until the end of the *ancien régime* the two styles enjoyed an enviably peaceful coexistence, even in the most elegant and luxurious residences, like that of the Duc de Choiseul. In one of the miniatures on his famous snuffbox there are a secrétaire and a bookcase in the classicising style of Oeben next to chairs and a bed in distinct Louis XV taste, while by the window can be distinguished the tentatively curving form of a commode *en tombeau* of the type usually called *à la Régence*. This is why one must be extremely cautious when dating a piece of furniture only according to stylistic criteria or on the basis of conjecture about 18th-century fashion and habits, for it is often far more complicated than it appears.

After a decade, in about 1775, the flourishing use of pictorial inlay began to die down in favour of geometrical decoration. This was only the beginning of a new simplicity of line which was soon to be encouraged by English influence, and by contacts with the young United States of America. Within a few years this severity was taken to its extreme, and while the exquisitely elegant proportions and accuracy of every detail were maintained, the imaginative inventiveness typical of the outstanding creations of the cabinet-makers until that moment gave way to the rather academic culture of the classicists.

The frequent use of mahogany in its natural state, to take advantage of its beautiful graining, characterised this period of Louis XVI, which was called the 'Etruscan style', because many designers had had recourse to antique vases which had been found mostly in Tuscany, and were considered indiscriminately to be Etruscan. The geometrical strictness of decoration and the uncluttered lines were emphasised by smooth, unadorned surfaces giving the surroundings a severe, chaste appearance allied to the new ideas of the painter David. He had a hand himself in these changes, designing models for several pieces of furniture of 'archaeological' character, which were realised by Georges Jacob, who, with Riesener, was the greatest cabinet-maker of the time. Unfortunately not one of his pieces is left, and one must be content to study them in some of the master's paintings, like the *Paris and Helen,* painted for the Comte d'Artois between 1786 and 1788, or the *Death of Socrates.*

There do exist, however, the three types of chair designed by Hubert Robert, another painter under

49. Louis XVI's library at Versailles.

50. Georg Haupt (1741-1784). Cabinet made for a
geological collection. 1774.

49. Louis XVI's library at Versailles. The room itself was designed by Gabriel, but it was executed by Antoine Rousseau. The beautiful bookshelves are separated at the corners by panels of allegorical motifs, and on top are busts of Roman emperors. The large table is the work of Riesener; the top is made of a single piece of sequoia. The roll-top desk in the background is by the cabinet-maker Roentgen.

50. Georg Haupt (1741-1784). Cabinet made for a geological collection. 1774. Musée Condé, Chantilly. The Swedish cabinet-maker Haupt had been trained partly in Paris in the workshop of Leleu, and had been a pupil of the famous Oeben. This piece is unique among 18th-century furniture for the extraordinary decoration of stones and rock-crystal on its top, as well as for its extreme elegance. It was given to the Prince de Condé by the King of Sweden.

51. Joseph Stöckel (1743-1802). Commode. Victoria and Albert Museum, London. This commode is of the crescent-shaped variety. It is the work of a cabinet-maker of German origin who worked consistently in Paris from 1769 and, as a result, had a definite importance in the formation of the Empire style. His works are always of very high quality and very lavish; on many occasions he made furniture for the Crown.

52. Balthazar Lieutaud (d. 1780). Clock. Wallace Collection, London. Veneered in oak and ebony and with superb bronze decoration this clock is particularly interesting because it shows sidereal and terrestrial time, as well as the date. It also has a barometer placed under the dial. The bronze serpent which encircles the face of the clock is a symbol of eternity.

51. Joseph Stöckel (1743-1802). Commode. Victoria and Albert Museum, London.
52. Balthazar Lieutaud (d. 1780). Clock. Wallace Collection, London.

52

the spell of the classical world, and executed by Jacob for the dairy of Rambouillet in 1787. Whatever the policy may have been which gave rise to the conception of these elegant copies of classical models it is forgotten when one sees how perfectly these pieces are made, limited, as they were, to absolute essentials. The result is in no way heavy—contrary to what certain commentators on the 18th century assert, some of whom seem blind to anything which is not a triumph of airy flourishes and jewelled ribbons. In fact there had been a presentiment of this virile austerity in the previous decade, and these pieces were the culmination of a gradual process. One need only think of the great jewel cabinet given to Marie Antoinette by Louis XV in 1770 on the occasion of the future Louis XVI's marriage. It was designed by Belanger and is one of the outstanding works of the career of the man who, as architect to the Comte d'Artois at Bagatelle, played a decisive role in the forming of the Etruscan style. On the other hand Riesener, the great cabinet-maker to the Crown, had completed as early as 1775 the first piece of furniture in solid mahogany for which there is a definite date, a commode for the use of the King when he visited his factory at Sèvres. The huge table, also in mahogany, originally intended for the King's library at Versailles, appears to have been made in the same year. Looking at its severe lines and its sober bronze decoration one cannot help being amazed at the thought that in the same year Riesener had produced one of the most elaborate pieces of furniture ever made, the commode for the King's bedroom at

Versailles, now in the Musée Chantilly, where the bronzes look as though they are sculpted in the round and the pictorial inlay is almost oppressive in its exuberance.

A brief look at the types of furniture most frequently found in late 18th-century interiors must start with the commode which was the great creation of the century. It made its debut at the end of Louis XIV's reign, became very popular during the Regency, under Louis XV assumed lighter, more curving shapes which gave it an exquisitely statuesque effect, and finally with the advent of Neo-classicism acquired more architecturally defined forms. In the commodes of the transitional period between Louis XV and Louis XVI, the legs are still curved in the Rococo manner, but soon they were straightened out or given shapes inspired in some way by classical forms, often finished in bronze and carved with flutings. The commode was covered with a marble top, underneath which was a long shallow drawer forming a sort of band or frieze often divided into three. Another characteristic of many Louis XVI commodes is the way the front is apparently divided into three sections. Usually the central part is slightly more prominent than the rest; this is almost always the case in the commodes made by Riesener, and is accentuated by a sober bronze decoration framing the central panel, which is often of trapezoid shape and elegantly inlaid. The commodes *à encoignures* were so called because of the two corner cabinets which fitted on to the sides of the commode to form one piece with it (an elegant example by Leleu is in

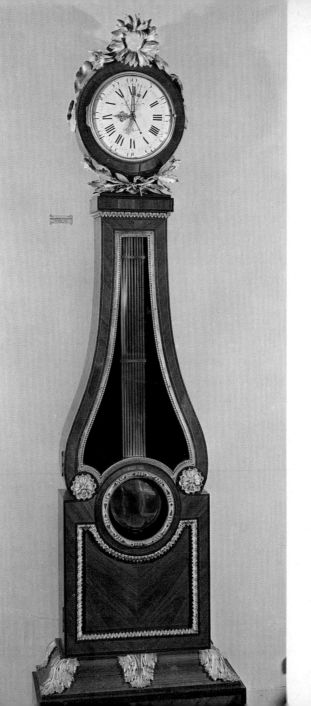

53

53. Nicolas Petit (1732-1791). Clock. Conservatoire des
Arts et Métiers, Paris.
54. Etienne Avril (1748-1791). Small cupboard. Fontainebleau.

53.   Nicolas Petit (1732-1791). Clock. Conservatoire des Arts et Métiers, Paris. Although Petit began his career as a cabinet-maker making Rococo commodes, he later became one of the first heralds of the Greek style. This *régulateur* with the mechanism by Lepaute belongs to his later phase.

54.   Etienne Avril (1748-1791). Small cupboard. Fontainebleau. This little mahogany piece reveals a certain English influence in its very severe lines. The austerity is partly relieved by the beautiful Sèvres biscuit medallions and by the delicate gilt bronze mounts. It is presumed from one of the marks to have belonged to the Queen, perhaps at the Château of St Cloud, for which Avril had produced other work.

55.   Guillaume Benneman (active at the end of the reign of Louis XVI and until about 1800). *Bureau plat.* Louvre, Paris. The unquestioned success of this cabinet-maker, who supplied the court for a long time after Riesener's disgrace in 1784, has been somewhat impaired by recent studies which have revealed that he was more a clever craftsman than a real artist. This piece belonged to Louis XVI and used to be in the library at Compiègne. The bronzes which decorate it are by Thomire.

56.   Guillaume Benneman (active at the end of the reign of Louis XVI until about 1800). Commode. Louvre, Paris. This magnificent commode was originally made by Stöckel for the Comte de Provence; a few years later, after 1786, Benneman under Haure's direction transformed it for Louis XVI's bedroom at Compiègne. Veneered in mahogany, it is particularly remarkable for its bronze doves and the bow and quiver of Love.

55. Guillaume Benneman Bureau plat. Louvre, Paris.

56. Guillaume Benneman (active at the end of the reign of Louis XVI until about 1800). Commode. Louvre, Paris.

the Wallace Collection). Those *à vantaux* have drawers concealed by doors, as in the superb piece by Martin Carlin in the Louvre, which is decorated with lacquer panels, and also has two open corner cabinets backed with mirrors for displaying *objets d'art*. These two types of commode already existed in the previous reign and only had to be adapted to the new classicism. Besides these there was a third type of commode which was particularly popular at this period, the crescent-shaped commode, a particular favourite of the cabinet-maker Stöckel.

A commode can measure as much as nine feet long, but there are some that are so much smaller, like the ones by Leleu in the Petit Trianon, that they are called demi-commodes. One special type was made out of Chinese lacquer boxes which may have had as many as ten or twelve drawers of different sizes in order to use a complete set of these precious objects. When, on the other hand, the seven drawers are arranged on top of one another thus making a piece much taller than a normal commode, it is called a *chiffonier* (the name *semainier* by which it is known today is a modern term). If the commode has no drawers but only shelves concealed by doors, is more sturdy in appearance and with shorter legs, it is called *meuble à hauteur d'appui, bas d'armoire* or cabinet. One particular type of cabinet resting on very tall legs is the jewel cabinet, which was obviously very rare as it was only made for the court and for the most important nobles. However, other types exist which were used as coin cabinets, or intended to contain specific collections, and which were the last descendants of the 17th-century *Wunderkammer*. The one presented by King Gustav III of Sweden to the Prince de Condé in 1774 for his collection of minerals is particularly famous, an extraordinary work by the Swedish cabinet-maker G. Haupt, which is illustrated in Plate 50 as an example of how 18th-century French art had spread throughout Europe. Even on the outside, which is in the form of a large wall-secrétaire, the purpose of the piece is evident from the magnificent inlay depicting a torch and various mineralogical tools. Even more obvious is the crowning arrangement of minerals and rock crystals in their natural state, an idea only encountered in this piece.

Particularly in vogue during Louis XVI's reign was the console, a *meuble à hauteur d'appui* to be fixed to a wall, in which the decoration usually matched the *boiseries*. Consoles are usually supported on only two inward-curving legs, but there is a type of commode console which is simply a commode with no drawers or doors, but with shelves instead for displaying works of art, or in the dining room for plates and platters. The table which was still most popular for office use was the *bureau plat*. It was rectangular and stood on four legs, which were always straight at this period and were often decorated with fluting, lictor's fasces, or ornamental bronzes. Usually it was covered with morocco leather fastened round the edges with a narrow gilt bronze frame, and had beneath the top a series of two or three very shallow drawers and various small flaps which could be pulled out if more space was needed.

57. Jean François Leleu (1729-1807). Commode. 1772.
Wallace Collection, London.

58. René Dubois (1737-1799). Commode. Wallace
Collection, London.

59. Louis XVI bed à la polonaise. *c.* 1785. Musée Cognacq-Jay, Paris.

57. Jean François Leleu (1729-1807). Commode. 1772. Wallace Collection, London. When the commode (of the type called *à encoignures*) was given to the Prince de Condé by Leleu in December 1772 it had a beautiful inlay on a blue background with the monogram of the Prince. Under the Revolution all that decoration was removed, leaving only the *fleurs de lys* of the gilt bronze frieze. The veneer is mahogany on oak.

58. René Dubois (1737-1799). Commode. Wallace Collection, London. This commode is of the type called en console because it rests on two tall legs and has only one drawer. It is veneered in purple-wood, dyed black, and decorated with extraordinary bronzes of sirens with two tails, with doves (symbols of conjugal love) and with lacquer panels. Dated about 1765, it is one of the earliest examples of Neo-classical furniture.

59. Louis XVI bed à la polonaise. *c.* 1785. Musée Cognacq-Jay, Paris. The bed is upholstered in the same fabric as the canopy above, which is hung with rich silk curtains held up by invisible supports and draped over classical style poles. The wooden parts of the bed are not so important. Like many Neo-classical style beds it would be placed lengthwise against the wall.

60. Jean Henri Riesener (1734-1806). Commode. Musée Nissim de Camondo, Paris. This commode may be dated about 1770. Its bronzes are of a magnificent quality such as are often found on the furniture made by Marie Antoinette's cabinet-maker. The superb pictorial inlay on the central panel is particularly impressive; the side panels have a more typical geometrical and diamond-shaped decoration which is found in many other works by this craftsman.

60. Jean Henri Riesener (1734-1806). Commode.

The *bureau plat* had its logical complement in the *cartonnier,* a little piece of furniture made of leather boxes which could be rested on one side of the table. Obviously ladies' writing tables were much smaller and in many cases embellished with all sorts of precious decoration, fine bronzes, lacquer, ebony and other rare materials, like the little writing table by Weisweiler reproduced in Plate 43. In cases like this, where the object is more like a jewel than a piece of furniture, it is fitting to remember the role played by the *marchands merciers*—halfway between the antique dealer and the decorator of our time—who supplied the court and often superintended the making of the most important pieces. After Louis XV the fall-front desk went out of fashion almost entirely, its place being taken by the roll-top desk, of which the first and most important example was made for the King between 1760 and 1769 by Oeben and Riesener. This desk, which was also called *à la Kaunitz* because of the tradition which attributed its creation to Maria Theresa's ambassador, had enormous success as much for its usefulness as for its pleasing appearance. The exquisite piece that Riesener made for the Queen's boudoir at Fontainebleau, illustrated in Plate 63, shows what these desks were like. The normal *bureau plat* has an upper part which is closed by a sort of semicircular portcullis; this is pushed up and back to uncover a series of little drawers and a sliding panel which can be used as a convenient writing desk. The roll-top desk was finished on all sides, and could thus be placed in the middle of the room or by a window, but the fall-front desk, which is more compact and taller, stood against the wall. In the latter a drop flap closed the upper part, hiding the shelves and little drawers, and providing ample writing space when lowered. Two doors in the lower part concealed more compartments and drawers, and sometimes even a safe. The desk was usually finished on top by a long shallow drawer decorated like a frieze on the outside and topped, as in commodes and corner cabinets, by a slab of marble, which they tried to match up with the marble of the mantlepieces. Occasionally in this period four very long legs were substituted for the lower half, as in the example, reproduced in Plate 64, by Martin Carlin, which is in the Metropolitan Museum, and is decorated with beautiful plaques of Sèvres porcelain. It is impossible here to list in an exhaustive way all the different types of table which were found during the Louis XVI period, and many of them were only the established models of the previous reign brought up to date. There was the *bonheur du jour,* for writing and also for the *toilette,* a little luxury object, always richly decorated and surmounted by a top part with little doors and tiny drawers. There was the secrétaire *à la Bourgogne,* also for writing, where the little drawers and compartments were concealed under the lift-up lid. Then there was the one called *à la Tronchin,* which was even more convenient as the top could be moved to various heights, by a system of levers, so that it could be used as easily standing as sitting down.

Among the even smaller models were the little tables *en chiffonier,* which are miniature editions of commodes with unusually tall legs. The *vide poches*

61. Jean Henri Riesener (1734-1806). Small writing table
Louvre, Paris.

62. Reconstruction of a Louis XVI interior. Musée Nissim de Camondo, Paris.

61.   Jean Henri Riesener (1734-1806). Small writing table. Louvre, Paris. Even in his less important furniture Riesener's art always attains an excellent level of quality. This lady's writing table, for example, is particularly striking for its impeccably graceful proportions, for the unerring precision with which the bronzes are grafted on to the top of the legs, and for its exquisite inlays.

62.   Reconstruction of a Louis XVI interior. Musée Nissim de Camondo, Paris. The two low chairs by the fireplace are particularly interesting. They are voyeuses made by the cabinet-maker J. B. Sené for the Turkish Room of the Château de Montreuil in 1789. The bergère in the background is by Chevigny, and the commode next to it is by Leleu. The fire-screen has a small Beauvais tapestry designed by Oudry, who also designed the large tapestry on the left made at the Aubusson factory.

63.   Marie Antoinette's boudoir at Fontainebleau. The beautiful gold and silver harmony of this boudoir was created in 1785 by Rousseau. Riesener made the two pieces of furniture seen here, a roll-top desk and a small work table, using mother-of-pearl for the veneer, and gilt and silver bronze and steel for the mounts. The chairs, which are no longer *in situ,* were by Jacob.

64.   Martin Carlin (d. 1785). Secrétaire. Metropolitan Museum, New York. This is a superb example of the furniture decorated with porcelain plaques, which was quite often found towards the end of Louis XV's reign and was favoured by Madame du Barry. Made by Carlin, this secrétaire can be dated 1773, as the marks of the porcelain decoration are of that year.

64. Martin Carlin (d. 1785). Secrétaire.

were often furnished with a little fire-screen, and with one or two shelves which little railings transformed into trays to hold all sorts of trinkets—snuffboxes, watches, pillboxes, bottles for smellingsalts etc. The little night tables, or *tables de chevet,* sometimes with sash frames, or hinged frames, had marble tops on which hot drinks could be placed. The tea-tables, or *guéridons,* stood on a three-footed pedestal and also had marble tops; the oval or kidney-shaped tables were for individual dining and occasionally for writing, and the *servantes* used to be placed next to every guest and were often furnished with metal containers to chill bottles. Finally there were the various work tables which provided for the contemporary craze for writing with a little panel which could be pulled out to rest on a drawer containing all the necessary writing materials, and of course there were many styles of games tables, which often had different tops for the various games. In some cases by lifting one or two panels the inside could be used for games like backgammon. In the *toilettes* the top is divided into three sections which lift up; the side panels open outwards and the centre flap opens back on itself, revealing the mirror on its under side. Dining tables appeared in France quite late, under English influence; they were usually in mahogany and could be made longer by means of a system of rods and additional sections. In the great pendulum clocks or *regulateurs* entrusted to specialist cabinet-makers, of whom the most famous was Balthazar Lieutaud, the shape was dictated to a certain extent by the length of the weights, but the decoration followed the same stylistic trend as other furniture. The example by Lieutaud in Plate 52, admirably adorned with gilt bronze mounts and topped by a garlanded vase in the style of Delafosse, also has the peculiarity of having a barometer set below the clock face.

Armchairs and seats offered little that was new, at least in their function and shape, as their basic characteristics had been established during the reign of Lous XV. But the decoration was adapted to suit the new trends in fashion, legs were naturally straighter, and the armrests, which no longer had to be moved back out of the way of unusually full skirts, were returned to their normal positions. The distinction was still made between *fauteuils meublants,* or armchairs with straight flat backs for ranging along the walls, which were only rarely sat on, and the *fauteuils courants,* with the curved backs *en cabriolet,* which were placed together in the centre of the room for conversation. It was in the latter that changes were most evident, as the backs were given all sorts of different shapes—medallion, horseshoe, and a trapezium-shape flanked by two slender little columns. In 1783 the backs of some of the chairs were even shaped like balloons as a tribute to the Montgolfier brothers' famous adventures. Influenced by the English, Jacob replaced the upholstered back of certain small mahogany chairs with a lyre shape. Jacob was the most original cabinet-maker of his day, although he should really be called a *menuisier,* the term the French use to describe the makers of chairs, beds and all types of furniture which was not inlaid.

He was the man, too, who invented the extraordinary Egyptian-style chairs which were later to reappear, very little changed, under the Empire. The three most common types of chair were the *bergère* with padded sides and a moveable cushion, the *cabinet* chair with an all-enveloping back and legs often arranged in a lozenge shape, and the *toilette* chairs, which were like the *cabinet* chairs, but had lower semicircular backs. There are also three types of *voyeuse*, which served a curious purpose, one in particular where one knelt or sat the wrong way round, resting one's elbows on the top of the back, which was padded for the purpose. Footstools still had their place, even if only for 'kings and cobblers', as S. Mercier sarcastically remarked, but by now their function was almost entirely decorative, as they were no longer a sign of social distinction.

The various types of Louis XVI divan did not differ from the traditional ones, the *canapé* was the most usual, with a back and armrests, while in the sofa the wooden parts were entirely hidden by upholstery, and the *sultane* had no backrest, but only two very high side panels. In the ottoman, which has only one side panel, the back is extended to curve round the other side. The *turquoise* was a sort of day-bed with sides and back of the same height. The *confident* was a small *canapé*, today called a *marquise*, which only seated two people. Finally the *chaise-longue* or *duchesse* was a long *bergère* ending in a sort of facing *bergère* for a footrest. When this was made as a single piece it was called *en bateau*, and when composed of two or three pieces a *duchesse brisée*.

65. Martin Carlin (d. 1785). Commode. Louvre, Paris.

66. André Louis Gilbert (1746-1809). Commode. Private collection, Paris.

67. Fall-front desk. Private collection, Paris.

65. Martin Carlin (d. 1785). Commode. Louvre, Paris. This commode was made for the Château de Bellevue, and is still decorated with oriental lacquers, although in style it is entirely Louis XVI. It is a commode *à encoignures,* but here the corner pieces are open for displaying curios and *objets d'art.*

66. André Louis Gilbert (1746-1809). Commode. Private collection, Paris. The decoration of the front of the commode is divided into three sections, which take no account of the horizontal division of the two large drawers. There are three smaller drawers below the marble top. The legs are still curved, as in all commodes of transitional style.

67. Fall-front desk. Private collection, Paris. The main decoration of this piece is the marquetry, which is of stylised flowers in diamond-shaped frames of purple-wood. The part played by the bronze mounts is much less important, as they are only used to round off the corners under the marble slab and for the little feet which are still in Louis XV style.

68. Louis XVI style divan. Rijksmuseum, Amsterdam. This divan, which bears no mark, is reminiscent of the style of Sené and Jacob on the eve of the Revolution. It is in a magnificent state of preservation. Not only is the original blue-and-white paintwork untouched, but its magnificent silk upholstery and the trimmings are intact.

68. Louis XVI style divan.

The most usual form of bed in Louis XVI's time is the one called *à la d'Artois,* which is placed lengthwise against the wall from which hangs its rectangular or square canopy. In the *à la polonaise,* on the other hand, the canopy is one with the bed, and its supporting columns can be seen, while the upper part is entirely covered by the hangings. *Duchesse* beds were very frequent and were placed in the usual way, with the canopy fixed to the wall. The type called *à l'anglaise* can only be distinguished from the *turquoise* by its larger size. Beds were usually in alcoves covered with mirrors or hangings.

The upholstery covering chairs, beds and divans continued to play a decisive part in the appearance of interiors. Silks, damasks and velvets were the most prevalent, but, besides these, new cotton materials and *toiles de Jouy* were becoming more popular. Leather was usually employed for covering *cabinet* chairs, and the Beauvais and Gobelins tapestries, which are today found on many 18th-century chairs, seem to have been used only rarely in that century. One of the aristocracy's delights was petit point embroidery, and Madame Elisabeth, the King's sister, with the help of her ladies covered the magnificent chairs by Boulard, which adorned her sitting room in the Château de Montreuil (Plate 38). There were also the silks embroidered by hand by the Queen herself for the beautiful suite by Sené now in the Metropolitan Museum, New York. These precious witnesses of the taste of a period still existed until about forty years ago when the silk was thoughtlessly replaced with a banal modern fabric.

The habit of having miniature models in wax to submit to clients was widespread. Some still exist, like the little bed in the Lefuel collection, made of three seashells intertwined with garlands of vine-leaves and crowned with a sumptuous canopy where a wreath of myrtle and roses encircles a pair of turtle doves. This bed, intended for Madame du Barry, was made in 1772 in wood, gold and silver and decorated with tapestry in *gros de Tours* embroidered on a white background with silk fringes and green trimmings. The bed no longer exists; in fact nothing more was heard of it after 1774 when Louis XV died. So his favourite, like the Venus of the doves in her shell, must have slept there for only two years before being finally driven from the court by the hatred of Marie Antoinette and the prudishness of the new sovereign. All to no avail: soon the *sans culottes* were to arrive and scatter the glory that had been Versailles. One can almost hear the last words of the divine countess: 'A moment more, executioner, a moment more'.

LIST OF ILLUSTRATIONS   Page